AN INTERVIEW *with* MY GRANDPARENT
A Sociological Examination

Yaffa A. Schlessinger

Hunter College of the City University of New York

The McGraw-Hill Companies, Inc.
Primis Custom Publishing

*New York St. Louis San Francisco Auckland Bogotá
Caracas Lisbon London Madrid Mexico Milan Montreal
New Delhi Paris San Juan Singapore Sydney Tokyo Toronto*

McGraw·Hill

A Division of The McGraw·Hill Companies

Editor: Adam Knepper
Manuscript Design and Preparation: Jakarta Eckhart, NiteOwl Creations
Copyeditor: Joseph F. Murphy
Cover Design: Maggie Lytle
Printer/Binder: Book-Mart Press, Inc.

table of contents   page

Introduction

Section I—Marriage and the Family 1

The title of this paper is Grandfather's Sketch, with details on life
in a village in Uganda

Some papers were selected for their historical landscape, others
for the story they tell. These two papers were selected for por-
traying the unconventional character of grandmothers who are
glamorous.

Two reports of traditional family life in British Guiana.

Arranged marriage and a wedding in China.

A fleeting romance of an Irish family in Bensonhurst, Brooklyn.

Attachment and separation in conflict in a Chinese family.

When "grandfather and grandmother had a huge argument."

A lighthearted love story of how grandfather met grandmother
when the heart was young and the pocket empty.

Introduction
Grandparent and Sociology

I n my many years of teaching "The Sociology of the Family," "Life Cycle" and "Youth and Adulthood," I never came upon a comprehensive study of the changing role of grandparents. In the course of time textbooks added new chapters on single parents, feminism, age and aging (as they did on death and dying), but the indexes had no references to grandparents and their relationships to any members of the family.

The recent *Sociological Abstract* of the American Sociological Association lists hundreds of research papers presented during the days in August 1997 when more than 4,700 sociologists convened for their annual meeting (footnotes, September/October 1997, p. 1). Nineteen pages of brief subject index list all the research papers. "Race and Ethnicity," and "Feminism" lead the way in the number of entries, about seventy for race—and if you add ethnicity the list grows much longer—and forty for feminism. There is one entry on age, one on ageism and only one on grandparents. I examined many catalogs of publishers, university press and others, that reach academic desks, and read carefully their titles and descriptions of chapters in the books. The grandparents are nowhere in sight. Even in titles on identity, a peculiar indigenous and persisting topic of modern man, the grandparents are absent.

Of all the books on the family that came my way, I remember the excellent ethnographic study by Young and Willmott, *Family and Kinship in East London*, (Penguin, New York, 1957), in which they discuss working-class families and the advantage of the proximity of three generations when grandparents help in caring for children. The advantage of the local kin system was broken when small families, given new housing, were then separated from their kin. The new building developments might have provided better dwellings with modern facilities, but mothers who found themselves far from the grandmothers suffered, as did the children. "In the three-generation family the burden of caring for the young, though bound to fall primarily on the mother, can be lightened by being shared with the grandmothers. The three generations complement each other." Once separated, the wives are left without the help of the grandmothers, and the old without the comfort of children and grandchildren (p. 197). I also remember a radio interview many years ago with Arthur Sulzberger, the then owner and chief editor of the *New York Times*, who had just returned from Communist China. He told his listeners that in China parents often chose to leave their children in the care of their grandmother rather than send them to a free daycare center provided by the government, which confirmed again the power of tradition in the affairs of man and the high value of the family in Chinese society.

The American Family Data Library offers what it claims to be state-of-the-art research data from the American Family Data Archive (Sociometrics Corporation, Los Altos, California, 1993), available in over 20,000 variables on CD-ROM. The subjects include National Survey of Families and Households, Childcare, Parents and Children, Low

Income Sub-Study, Marital Instability, Child Custody and National Family Violence Survey. No Grandparents in sight. The absence of grandparents from our textbooks and research on the family reflects the reality of contemporary family life. When the assignment to write on grandparents was introduced in class, many students had no grandparents to interview, and some did not know where their grandparents were born.

This small book brings the grandparents in. It does not offer a systematic research based on statistical or ethnographic data. But assigning the interviews made each student an active participant in studying the topic on a personal level. The interviews are an unassuming small research project (to be discussed later) that gives a picture of the grandparents' lives and their relationships their grandchildren.

GRANDPARENTS AS IMMIGRANTS

We are fortunate to have at Hunter College many students whose grandparents are immigrants. Their stories from many countries allow different and interesting accounts, and a comparative view. Auguste Comte (1789–1857), the French sociologist who gave sociology its name, believed that comparison was an integral part of doing sociological research. Comparison makes us see things that were not noted when viewed alone. It highlights that which was invisible and taken for granted.

I recently visited a home of two art collectors, a well-traveled husband and wife who were fascinated by masks, jars, woven fabrics and small and larger pieces of sculpture as well as drawings and paintings—each one unique and original, all of them interesting, most of them magnificent. As the hostess guided me through the many art pieces of the collection she said, "These artists were simple folks. They were not famous men, and they did not sign their names. Even in their own time and place they were not always given special honor often granted to great artists. Yet, they were very talented, and what they created is really wonderful." I remembered this as I read the papers of my students interviewing their immigrant grandparents, which I felt were interesting and often moving.

Immigrants are not a representative random sample of the group and country from which they come. Immigrants are self-selected strongly motivated people who found enough resources to get up, leave their homes and come to the United States. Those resources can be family ties, money, education, information and personal inner resources such as courage and ability to take risks and stand hardships. These people, many of whom were poor and illiterate, are high achievers. Their grandchildren managed to become students in good standing, at Hunter College of the City University of New York.

Although the United States is a land of immigrants, our history shows a regular pattern of anti-immigration laws shifting from old quota systems to favoring of family members of people already in the United States. A continuous research and debates about the cost and benefit of immigration argue both ways. The National Academy of Science, a nonprofit organization of distinguished scholars, published a four-hundred-page report on the effects of immigration on the economy of the United States.

The topic of immigration is often heated and controversial with political and economic arguments, a testimony of open aggression that interprets the same data in more than one way as it examines the economic factor of caring and educating immigrant children or recognizes the richness of the experience they add to American culture. Are the immigrants and their children a burden that will drain the American society, or are they a rich resource of human capital, youth, vitality, energy and broad cultural horizons?

The first settlers of the sixteenth century were mostly English and French. The nineteenth century brought a new influx of immigrants: Irish, Germans and Scandinavians, followed by Jews, Italians and Slavs. During the twentieth century new waves of immigrants from Asia, Africa and Central America, the Caribbean and the Middle East changed the complexion of the American population (*A Land of Immigrants*, David M. Reimers, Chelsea House Publishers, New York, 1996). In the nineteen-fifties the three top countries of origin were Germany, Canada and the United Kingdom. Today half of all immigrants come from Mexico, the Philippines, Vietnam, the Dominican Republic, Mainland China and Taiwan, Korea and India. The country's racial makeup is being altered. In 2050, according to the Academy study, the population of the United States will be 51 percent white, 14 percent black, 26 percent Hispanic and 8 percent Asian (*The New Yorker*, July 14, 1997 p. 41).

The interviews with the grandparents have become unintentionally a study of immigrants who ended up in the City of New York. Since New York City is not the United States, we took care to give the large picture of immigration to the United States.

an interview with my grandparent

One of the important trends of contemporary art, in all forms, is its moving away from the temples and palaces, moving toward secularization and democratization. The images of the Madonna and Christ-on-the-Cross gave way to mundane images of the shovel by Jim Dine, the urinary by Marcel Duchamp, soup cans by Andy Warhol. In the world of drama *Oedipus* by Sophocles and *Hamlet* by Shakespeare gave way to Willie Loman by Arthur Miller and the saloon life of the waterfront with the colloquial language of fallen men and women of Eugene O'Neill or Tennessee Williams. In music Lincoln Center is bringing in popular music as part of its regular programs and the Queens Symphony Orchestra is doing the same as the audience for classical music has fallen dramatically throughout the country.

In the world of literature this trend has been manifested by a flood of autobiographies. Perhaps talk shows are the echo of this phenomenon. Maureen Dowd, in her *New York Times* column (March 15, 1997), told us that of the top eleven books then on the *Times* nonfiction best-seller list nine were autobiographical—from Katharine Graham of the *Washington Post* to Kathryn Harrison, author of "The Kiss" (a story of the four-year consensual love affair between a twenty-year-old daughter and her father).

Letters to the editor soon followed. *New York Times,* March 21, 1997: "Memoir writing is not just about telling your story. It is about figuring out that you are the person you are because of your experience. By doing this you have the power to transform your life and the lives of others." Another letter said: "Autobiography and memoir provide an unmatched entry into the individual's struggle with the possibilities and diminishment of existence... Our age's deadly combination of cultural flatness and personal disjunction renders many of us the beleaguered wayfarers in need of some secular clues. Autobiography, performed authentically, often provides one."

Tobias Wolff, in a *New York Times* Op-Ed piece of April 6, 1997, noted that often writers of memoirs "exploit those who trusted them, betrayed intimacies, displayed their wounds in the market place... . The autobiographer is bound to puff himself up, to lie, to make revenge, to hide the greater sin by confessing the lesser, to crown herself in a halo." But the best memoir writers "have an astonishing capacity for seeing themselves in the round, fully implicated in the fallen creation of which they write."

Comparing the arts of letters with the visual arts, an autobiography with self-portrait, one realizes the rich contribution of the self-portrait to the art of the Western world. "Rembrandt's self-portraits made at the end of his life are, for many people, the apex of Western art. Here after a lifetime of painting for clients, he seems to be working only to please himself, to record the falling away of his flesh, an artist's self-control in the grip of death. His face—eyes brimming with sadness and hope—has become the image, sentimentally corrupted by Hollywood, of what old age should be. He is what wisdom looks like: mature, sober, melancholic view of life" *(New York Times,* January 22, 1989, p. 35).

Add to it this portraits by great artists of the people they loved, mothers, wives, fathers, children and other members of the family: Dürer, 1514; Morisot, 1869; Whistler, 1871; Gorky, 1882; Hockney, 1982. The value of the work was never determined by the subject matter, and the profound feelings the artists had toward their subjects never diminished the value of the work of art. One is reminded of the mailman who delivered the mail to Van Gogh in the asylum. So moving are these paintings that I have tried to collect them in postcards whenever I find them in museum shops.

Suzanne K. Langer *(Current Biographies,* 1963, p. 235) argues that the artist seeks not to arouse or convey feelings, but to portray the nature of feelings. "A work of art possesses a conception of life, emotion, inner reality, but it is neither confessional nor a frozen tantrum; it is a developed metaphor, a non-discursive symbol that articulates what is verbally ineffable." Not the artist's own actual feelings, but what the artist knows about human feelings.

hIstoRy anò bIogRaphy

Can such an autobiography, expressed as an oral document, an interview or a written essay, be considered history?

It has been observed that history has been written by the winners, by rulers of nations and men of power. Studs Terkel, whose literary work depends on interviews, noted (on radio station WNYC, September 20, 1991) that these men of power then claim that they built the pyramid, China's Great Wall and the Taj Mahal and call their version history. All the people who participated in these great events are not mentioned, not given credit and, worst of all, not given a voice. Kurt Weill, in one of his poems, refers to King Philip of Spain who wept after the fall of the Armada in the Spanish war against England. Were there no other tears, Weill asks? The current controversy of the new exhibit about the German army and its behavior during World War II reflects the heated argument between two versions of historical events. Yet there is often someone from the losing camp who survived to tell the tale. Bottom-up history, Terkel calls it. More and more historians resort to this view. Slavery in America is one engaging topic. Long neglected, it is now being studied from the bottom-up point of view. The grandparents' stories present lives of simple people whose names are not found in any history book. Even those who argue that heroes make history will agree that their power to change the world is ultimately manifested or validated in the changing lives of simple folks, ordinary people. The past is alive to the degree that it has become a part of the lives of living people. The past exists in the present. Through the interview the memory of the grandparent has become part of the memory of the grandchild, the student who conducts the interview. As Mary Douglas (Maurice Halbwachs, *The Collective Memory,* Harper and Row, New York, 1980, Introduction) notes about Durkheim's idea of collective consciousness, the experience of the individual is linked to the community to which he or she belongs—a moral community with its own membership and allegiance. Listening to these stories of the grandparents, most of whom are immigrants, one realizes the shifts of communities and allegiances they experienced. The commitment to a life-style and a way of life illuminates the conflict between the two worlds, or between the generations.

ınterview as an art form

Can an interview be an art form? In these interviews both students who conducted them and grandparents who responded were not professional in any way. At best the work can be considered folk art, like folk dance, folk music and quilts. As Howard Becker (*Art Worlds*, University of California Press, Berkeley, 1982) tells us, folk art is linked to the community more than to the production of professional pieces of art. At times the work may express sophisticated style, original vocabulary and an interesting angle of vision, but it has not been created by professional artists, or for the purpose of creating a perfect artistic work with commercial value. The local neighborhood and the local community are the audience for which it has been produced, usually as a way to remember, as a way to celebrate. Becker quotes a woman who told how when she was a little girl she helped her mother in quilting. Her father thought that the child's large stitches ruined the quilt. But her mother insisted that those stitches were going to stay until the quilt was worn out—a wonderful anecdote conveying the main purpose of the quilt, which was often made out of leftover material, a remnant loaded with memories. Sometimes such a piece will evoke a whole childhood, a time, a place, a happy event for which the dress had been made. The whole quilt represents such events which together make a total picture of a life as documented by the pieces that make the quilt. Until recently, no artist has signed his name to a quilt. The memorial quilt which has become a tradition in the gay community to commemorate its losses to AIDS is a direct development from the original quilt, made to give warmth or as a decorative piece, a bedspread.

The quilt as an art form is very different from the tapestries which were made for palaces, designed by artists like Goya and Rubens. Yet many of the women who participated in making the tapestries knew how to stitch skillfully, but did not consider themselves artists or leave their names on their work. As in all other human affairs, it is hard to draw clear lines between folk artists and professional artists in all areas of art. The poet Walt Whitman, the novelist Theodore Dreiser, and the dancer Bob Fosse are examples of great artists who started without professional training. The collection of the grandparent interviews resembles the quilt. Unrelated interviews, when put together, give a total picture, a gestalt impression; the whole is larger than the sum of the parts. Even when no connection can be found among the interviews, the disjunction is significant in its own right, an important statement about American society, made of immigrants, whose lives came to a proximity pretty much like the quilt and created a curious design. So near by, so far apart, they create a new meaning with its own coherence, not a quilt with a repeated geometric design, marked by careful precision, but one that stitched together the many collected pieces accumulated through time by accident and not by preconceived design. Its major values lie in its charm, originality and authenticity.

man and society: the sociological perspective

This assignment has been given through the years at Hunter College in the course of "The Sociology of the Family." The benefits for the students have been many. In a personal way the students have been introduced to the sociological perspective as they realized firsthand that the people they interviewed lived in another time and another place, and were given different opportunities and different life choices. Sociologically, they have understood that the expectations were different, and so were the life choices and the aspirations. By doing the interviews they have learned the lesson of C. Wright Mills in his book *The Sociological Imagination* (Oxford University Press, New York, 1959) that the study of sociology is history and biography, personal problems and public issues. Often one finds it difficult to understand human behavior unless one learns the situation in which it occurred: the time and place.

The students have also learned in a very real way about the social change that went through the generations, and perhaps the personal gain and cost of that change. There is an emphasis on the gain and loss that every change brings about, and the interesting question: Who gained and who lost? The biography of Andrew Carnegie shows how the industrial revolution destroyed his father's cottage industry in Scotland and made Andrew Carnegie the richest man in the world in his time. Listening to our grandparents' stories, we see the dramatic differences between our own lives and theirs. We are also amazed at some things that persist, important things. Values die hard. The fact that many students had no grandparents to interview and that some did not even know where their grandparents came from explains the feelings of alienation that mark modern man. History makes us feel at home in the world, and these interviews were in some way about the students themselves. They were a revelation.

memories and self-image: a personal document

The students understood that this was not a testimony of what happened, to be presented in court. It was an interview given to a grandchild, a college student, for a class assignment. Memories are selective according to the purpose of their being remembered. The grandparent told his grandchild what he wanted him to hear. Goffman's theory of the "arts of impression management" comes to mind (*The Presentation of Self in Everyday Life,* Doubleday Anchor, New York, 1959, pp. 208–237). The grandparent who wanted to look good concealed and revealed selectively. He created his memories as much as he remembered them; he is an active actor who has a stake in the image he projects and how he wants people to think about him. But what is looking good? How does he want to be remembered? The interview was an

expression of the values of the times, of the personal reflec-
tion and personal feelings of one's life and one's image.
Almost all the interviewees (almost, for there were few
students who wrote on wealthy families, and even those lost
their fortunes during the political upheavals) knew dire
poverty and hardworking parents. There was a streak of
nostalgia not for the hard times but for their childhood, for
their parents who had since died, for the countries they left
behind, most of all for the youth they remembered and the
fact that "they have made it." They wanted to remember the
poverty and the hard times so that the grandchild might
appreciate the success of the grandparent who got out of
poverty. The interview is more an expression of affection for
a grandchild, a college student, a far cry from what the
illiterate grandparent had been when he or she was the
student's age. The distance the grandparent traveled in one
lifetime, the differences between his grandparents and his
grandchildren, is astonishing. The American Dream did not
deceive him. And so the distortions of the voyage are part of
the memory, documents in their own right. Perhaps one of
the values of this paper is that it afforded the grandparent
and grandchild a chance to reflect together on a life journey
with gratitude.

Erik Erikson, in his book *Childhood and Society* (Norton,
New York, 1963), in the chapter "Eight Ages of Man," calls
the final stage of life "Ego Integrity vs. Despair." Erikson
describes the need of every man to find some sense of order
and meaning in the life he has left, to see it as a coherent
whole. Most important is the ability to accept disappoint-
ments and losses. "It is the acceptance of one's one and only
life cycle as something that had to be and that, by necessity,
permitted of no substitutions: it thus means a new, a different love of one's parents. It is comradeship with the ordering
ways of distance times and different pursuits" (p. 268).

Erikson ends the chapter with a very relevant point for this paper: closing the life cycle, he brings together two basic principles, one at the first stage of life, infancy, and the other at the end of old age. The first is trust, the last is integrity. Trust, says Erikson, is defined as the assured reliance on another's integrity. Thus infantile trust depends on the elder's integrity. This integrity and trust and their interconnection give us the courage to live and die (p. 26).

When Mother Theresa, the woman who dedicated her life to the poor and the sick, the suffering and the dying in India, died at the age of 86, one of the mourners related his own encounter. When he asked Mother Theresa what he could do, she sent him to comfort the dying. When the man he comforted died, she told him, "You did not know him, and now you are his son, you carry his memory," as if to imply that it is upon a son to carry his father's memory, as if it is the joy of a father to know that he left someone behind who will remember him.

Memories are selective. Many theories try to explain the key to the selective memory. What is it that we remember, and what do we forget. Freud believed that nothing that has ever happened to us perishes (*Civilization and its Discontent*, Norton, New York, 1962. p. 16). He observed that free association can trace back the memories and be beneficial. Often, memories are a burden. Pain and sorrow can be so disruptive that they make it impossible to carry on our daily lives. Cruel events had better be forgotten so we can move along. But the persistence of memories is not always easy to overcome. They go down to the unconscious, dynamic as ever. It is here that Freud believed we should bring them up so that we can better control them and go on with our lives.

Others testify that under extreme conditions they did not forget but tried to remember traumatic events. Maria Rosa Henson, (New York Times:, August 27, 1997, p. D19), victim of Japanese who forced her and other Philippine women into prostitution, and who was the first to step out to tell the story, said, "I am telling the story so that they may feel humiliated...I am avenger of the dead...I learned to remember everything, to remember always, so that I will not go mad."

Maurice Halbwachs, in his book *The Collective Memory* (Harper and Row, New York, 1980), noted that when we say, as we often do, I remember, we do not always refer to that which we experienced directly. Often we learned about an event we remember because someone had told us about it. We might have heard it on the radio, or read it in the paper, or seen it on television. Almost everyone remembers the death of President John Kennedy. We remember the time and place and the people who shared it with us. The impact of the event experienced indirectly was strong and unforgettable. Having experienced an event directly does not necessarily make the memory of it more accurate. Memories may be made of bits and pieces and we fill in what is missing to complete the picture or the story. It is like a fresco with great gaps where there is nothing but a brick wall and the fresco has gone forever. In the film *The Return of Martin Guerre*, based on a true story, two men claim that each one is Martin Guerre returning from the war. As they are questioned about events that happened in the community long before, the real Martin Guerre who was there at the time of the event forgets the details, the impostor who was his military buddy during the war and who heard the story remembers it well.

Stories heard are translated in our minds into images of our own, to fit our own psyche, and they engrave themselves in our memory deeply and clearly. They stay. Memories of the past exist to the degree that someone in the present remembers them (Mary Douglas, in Halbwachs, *The*

Collective Memory, 1980, Introduction). The fact that the interviewer was not a stranger but a grandson adds significance to the listening and recording, as it does to the remembering and telling. In transmitting this experience into a paper the interviewer creates a physical visible point of reference. The subjective memory becomes an object, a small monument, a recorded interview.

interview as a technique

What do we want to know and how are we going to ask the question? A delicate balance must be maintained. The balance between an open ending, allowing the best stories to come forth, and not letting the interview derail. William H. White told us that often in an interview, the interviewer has no patience to wait for an answer, and if it does not come forth immediately, the interviewer then helps along by repeating the question, explaining it or simply putting words in the mouth of the interviewee, according to expectations. The interviewer must be prepared to wait. Such moments of silence are an integral part of responding. Some used a tape recorder, others a pencil and paper. Still others did the interview on long-distance telephone. In an unstructured interview, an open-ended question is designed to permit the respondent to answer in his or her own terms, own frame of reference and own words. All the interviews reflected the human condition: people caught up by social forces beyond their control, and the personal freedom they exercised within these confines.

the organization of the papers

We resisted the temptation to organize the book according to the ethnic origin of the grandparents, although this would have been the clearest, easiest and simplest method. It seemed more appropriate to group the papers according to social institutions, though no paper addressed itself to one major theme by which we could place it unequivocally. Often it was difficult to decide whether to put a paper in the chapter on political systems or the economic one, family, religion or education.

This classification had its advantage. As papers of different ethnic groups were put in the same chapter, they allowed a dramatic comparison among the lives of people in different countries. Even the sound of the names introduced different images, different lifestyles and different cultural traditions. Style is an illusive concept, and so the distinctive names of Chinese, Spanish, Russian or African people who appeared in each paper helped evoke what was difficult to do in other words. The fact that the same paper could have easily belonged to the chapter on education or on political systems made clear the interconnection among all the institutions. The links between education and fertility and between economic and political systems are so strong that the lines are actually blurred.

Reading the papers, one learns about the difference between traditional and modern worlds, between rural and urban life, between educated and illiterate people, between poverty and advanced economy, between totalitarian and democratic political systems. The changing size of the family and the definition of sex roles are conveyed not on an abstract theoretical level but on the experiential level of daily life.

Often the style of the story conveys deep social values, in charm and grace. A Chinese woman tells her granddaughter that it is boastful to talk about oneself. Another grandmother simply does not express love or talk about sex as her modern grandchild does.

The narratives tell us about norms and values and roles of men and women and children and grandchildren in an experiential way. They tell us that every person is in some way like no other person, in some ways like some other persons and in some ways like all other persons.

This group of immigrants, the grandparents of college students, amaze us by the distance they traveled in literacy, in educational and economic achievements. In one lifetime, through their grandchildren, the grandparents crossed into different worlds, a testimony of their inner strength, which is maintained in the students' motivation and energy and sense of purpose. No one who reads these papers will fail to recognize the contributions these immigrants brought to the American shores.

section 1
marriage and the family

All the papers are really about family life, but some focus on the family exclusively. The unique attribute of the family is the combination of two basic principles: love and power (Kingsley Davis). The fact that the family is the first agent of socialization through which we become acquainted with the world, the frequency and intimacy which we experience in the family, the intense relationship, makes us vulnerable. We spend our childhood in the family where not only love but cruelty, too, is frequent. Murder and abuse, power and powerlessness, are just as common as love and growth. There is a particularly moving paper which speaks of conflict and cruelty within the family, where the child is caught between deep attachment to the grandmother and conflict with the mother. It is written with piercing rage and love expressed against the cultural background in which it occurred.

In Africa we still find polygamy, a mark of wealth and status, mostly among those who can afford it. We realize that in many traditional societies, arranged marriage still prevails. In such societies the family is more important than the individual, so it makes sense that the parents will select the new members who join the family. Marriage is an agreement between two families—not between two individuals—who come together in order to ensure the next generation. Perhaps the family is in a better position to make a wiser choice than the individual. Many young people from India who come to the United States for education return home with academic degrees and marry the person chosen by their parents. It may seem amazing that having been educated in Western society in American universities did not change their cultural norms of mate selection.

Another paper tells about a sleepy neighborhood and the life of a good simple man when a family of strangers with redheaded daughters throws a rock into his peaceful existence. The life of the simple man, the grandfather, is ignited with passion, but not for long. The redhead soon disappears, leaving her children behind, and the grandfather returns to a simple life of quiet loyalty and grace.

The interviews, many of which are not presented here, refuted the myth of "functional families." Divorce, desertion and single mothers are quite common, perhaps because they are still more frequent among poor people. Many of the families have many children and infant mortality is high. "My grandmother by the age of 24 had nine children…She learned to cook and clean when she was 9 years old." Of ten children, four die; of nine children, three die. One paper tells of a mother who had twelve children, two of whom died when they were so little that she did not remember their names. Still another grandmother killed her baby because she knew she could not feed the children she already had. In poor families the older daughter becomes "the big sister" and takes care of the younger ones. Almost all women work on the farm and go to the market to sell their produce or what they have cooked. Quite a few of the grandparents live to an old age of 80 or 90.

We end with glamorous grandmothers who defy the stereotype of old women. They love stylish clothes, beautiful perfumes, high-heeled sexy shoes. They are glamorous.

musisi k. kakumba

the purpose of this essay is to analyze my grandfather's sketch. In order to do that, I must examine several issues. These issues include my grandfather's childhood, parents, how he met my late grandmother, his marriage and what he remembers about my late grandmother.

I chose to do a biographic sketch of my grandfather on my father's side because my grandmother passed away last August. My grandfather grew up on a large farm like the rest of the boys in his village. On the farm he helped my great-grandparents to grow bananas, which is the staple food of my ethnic group, the Baganda. Since Uganda is located on the equator and has an altitude of 4,000 feet above sea level, it has many different seasons, in which people grow different crops. The cash crops grown on my grandfather's farm when he was a young boy were coffee, sugar, millet, beans, cotton and tobacco. During the food crop season he helped plant the banana trees, beans and millet. He also had to attend to the cattle, sheep and goats.

His day started at six o'clock in the morning, when he had to get up and help the milkman milk the cows. After helping the milkman, he would go and do some digging on his small farm; then after that he would go and dig on his parents' farm before going to school. He used to walk four miles to school every day. After school, he had to be home to fetch the water from the well, which was about one mile away. In addition to this he had to help in bringing the cattle, sheep and goats back from grazing.

My grandfather's parents, my great–grandparents, were very strict individuals. They raised my grandfather in a strict manner; he raised his children in the same way. He has five children, three boys and two girls. Since my grandfather grew up on a farm, he got married in a traditional way. People in most villages in Uganda do not date before marriage. They do not marry because of romantic love. People marry when the family and the community feel that the two people who plan to marry each other have reached marriage age. In my grandfather's village, marriage is a family and community affair.

When parents have a young lady that they want to marry off, they approach the parents of the young man to see if he is interested in their daughter. Once it has been established that the young man has accepted the young lady, there is a long process of negotiations on each side. After the negotiations, there is an exchange of gifts from the two sides; this means that an agreement has been reached. Then the young man's parents pay the "bride money."

It was through this lengthy process that my grandfather met and married my late grandmother. When I asked him what he remembered about my late grandmother, he said that she was a sweet, loving, caring and kind lady who cared very much for everybody in the village. When I asked him about the way life was when he was growing up compared to his present lifestyle, he said that life now is much easier. This is due to changes in time and advancements in modern technology. The last question that I asked my grandfather was whether he preferred the time when he was growing up or the modern times. He paused for a while and said that each time period has its advantages and disadvantages. When he was growing up, the community and the village helped him to grow.

Even though life was difficult, there was a sense of community togetherness. Life in the modern period is easier, but the sense of community togetherness is less. The village was the center of everything in the daily lives of its inhabitants. Today, the youth of the village are leaving, in search of modernity and its trappings in urban areas. As a result, the village is neglected. Sometimes this results in the loss of culture and custom for some people.

stacy mason

oma Edmonds was born on August 24, 1921, in Lawrenceville, Virginia, one of nine children. Her parents were Cora and Robert Edmonds. Her father was a farmer and her mother a housewife. Segregation played a big role in the times grandmother lived. She recalled that when she went to the bus station there was a section for colored and a section for whites. Food always played a part in grandma's life. She remembers how her mother used to cook on a coal stove. The foods they ate when they were younger remained the same through adulthood: collard greens, cabbage, all kinds of potatoes, fresh chicken and many other kinds of food you find on a farm. Grandma said there were many nights they went to bed hungry. The roads in those times weren't paved, just dirt, and the means of transportation was horses.

Doma turned 18 and that is when she fell in love. She married Clarence Mason and they had two children together, my father and his sister. After the birth of the two children, she decided to go to work.

When troubles began to brew in my grandparents' relationship, grandmother migrated to New York City with her two children. As soon as she arrived, she found a job in a department store. When grandma had saved enough money, she bought a house in the Bronx, and she still lives there. She also found a job in the Bronx. She worked in a hospital until she retired. When she moved to the Bronx, she met my step-grandfather.

My gram is one who loves to cook, and she is famous for her cabbage, roast beef and coconut custard pie.

Grandma can always be seen wearing six-inch heels with anything she wears, even sweat suits. For as long as I have known my grandmother, she has always dressed like a star. That's why her nickname is "Queenie." If you were ever around her, you would know that she is down- to-earth and a lot of fun.

myriam nau

my grandmother "Toute" (pronounced Toot) is
unique. She's 68 years old and behaves like a 40-
year-old woman. With a height of 6 feet 2 inches
she stands tall and erect. Her hair dyed jet black falls shiny
on her shoulders. Her nails are manicured and polished a
bright red. Her neck, ears, fingers, and arms are all adorned
with gold jewelry. She's wearing a silk pearl color robe with
matching slippers. She has an Indian complexion which
makes her seem tanned all year round. While I'm asking her
questions about her past, she walks around watering her plants
or stands by the window with a pensive look on her face.

The room is silent for a minute or two; then she sits
across from me and takes me for a ride into her past. Her
parents originated from the Dominican Republic and
crossed over to Haiti in the early 1900s. Her mother's name
was Olympe Oanasto and her father's name was Auguste
Soy. Both had Indian complexions with natural jet black
Indian hair. She was born in 1919 in the small town of
Belladere in Haiti. This town is situated near the border
separating Haiti and the Dominican Republic. She had three
brothers and three sisters. She is the sixth of the seven children her mother had. Times were hard while growing up in
the 1920s and 30s. There were depressions and wars in her

hometown. At night her father would gather all her brothers and sisters and tell them stories and jokes mostly to make them forget their misery and hunger. She was close to all her family members and loved them all. During those times they drank lots of tea and ate lots of cornbread. After the wars and depression simmered down, she went back to school. She walked almost four miles to school each day. She left home at dawn and returned after sunset. When at home she cleaned up, took care of the crops and performed all chores assigned to her. She tells me, "Unlike children today I didn't have to be told what to do a thousand times. I knew my duties." Although she lived in a nuclear family, many people were involved in her upbringing. Her neighbors and older family members were given the right to discipline her if she disrespected them or misbehaved. She says, "Respect was given to everyone and children obeyed their parents and elders. Children today lack discipline and are spoiled rotten. They didn't grow up in hardships or wars like I did, but I bet if they did they would behave differently and take life more seriously."

At the age of 16 she was sent by her parents to another town to live with her older sister, who was married to a police officer. She tells me, "I had to respect my brother-in-law like my own father." She lived with her sister for three years until she finished school at the age of 19. She went back home to help her parents with their household.

A month later, after Mass, her parents announced a visitor. She says, "This visitor became my husband." He was 40 years her senior. She says, "He was handsome, tall and also the mayor of our town." There was no time for court-ship because the minute he set eyes on her he immediately proposed. She had no say in this proposal because her parents beforehand had agreed to give up their daughter to this wealthy gentleman. Their decision was based on the prestige and comfortable lifestyle the marriage would bring to the family. She tells me, "I learned to love him. Although he had all the qualities a woman could ever want in a man, he would not have been my choice." She says, "Today's children are, in a way, better off than me. At least they get to choose their mate and make their own decisions." I tell her that it's still the same way with us, but not as obvious.

She had three children whom she raised on her own and without the supervision of a husband. He was too busy with politics. He gave her lots of money to take care of her house and their children until he died at the age of 93. After his death she felt both sad and liberated. She never remarried.

When I ask if she had a chance to change her past would she do it, her reply is a flat "no." With that "no" come several tear drops. I wait five minutes for another reply, but she says nothing. I end the interview and go over to her and give her a big hug. She is wearing Bal a Versailles, and that scent will remain in my memory for life.

Radhe Harnarain

my father, Bedassie, was born in 1885 in India. I do not know his other name. When he was about 18-20 years old, he had sneaked away from his family with two of his brothers and gone aboard a British ship harbored there. This ship took people to the far-off land— British Guiana, South America. Their parents had no idea they were gone until they were missing and the ship had already left. On their arrival in Guiana they had a three-year contract to work on the sugar estates of the county Blairmont. They could not break this contract. They lived in the lodges that the British had built to accommodate their laborers. After my father's contract ended, he left Blairmont and went to Rose Hall Town where he lived. He would work at Fort Mourant (the county next to Rose Hall). He then got married to Dani Besasar. She was born in 1890, I think, and was a third generation in Guiana. My mother had two sisters and three brothers. My father then bought a piece of land in Rose Hall. It was covered with bush and crabgrass. He built a mud-wall house with a zinc roof. Money was very hard to come by and he was very poor. People struggled to live and maintain their families. Most people could not afford zinc roofs and had grass roofs. My parents worked for eight cents per day. They planted cassava in the fields. My mother would grate the cassava, mix it with sugar and make pancakes. She would grind the rice and make flour which she used to make bake (a kind of bread).

My name is Sookrie Bedasie, and I was born on October 24, 1918, in British Guiana. I am the second of six children. When I was little, my parents sent me to school, but I did not like school. I could not go to school because I had to stay home to look after my brothers and sisters. There was no one to look after them and my parents had to work. My father had bought a donkey-cart in which he would go to the "water side" (woods and swampy area) to fetch firewood. This way he could bring a lot instead of a little bundle on his head. And he could bring the firewood faster because he had to go many miles for it. I remember my mother tying the gate with a long rope when she left us alone to go to work. She would tell us not to go outside. After she left we would try to untie it, but we could not do it. I remember us being very poor and not having nice clothes to wear. We would have clothes made from flour bags. (Flour came in cloth bags.) We would play in the water a lot and swim. We would take our clothes off and take mud and dab it along the bank of the river. Then we would sit on the bank and slide into the water. We did that a lot. [She lived next to the Atlantic Ocean.] I remember my father giving my mother a really hard time. After my sister and I were born, he asked my mother why she was having only girl children and not boys. He loved boy children. When I was about 16 years old, I got married. My father just went out one day to look for a husband for me. He met your Nana's father and told him that he heard that he [Goorsaran] had a son whom he would like for his daughter. [Nana is hindi for grandpa.] So it was arranged that Sookrie Bedasie would marry Laljie Goorsaran. Your Nana was born in Guiana and his father was also from India. They came to see me one day. I saw your Nana only once before we got married. We could not go out like people nowadays do before they get married. Your Nana was born on August 29, 1915. He was 20 years old when we got married in May 1936. I never disagreed with getting married. I never even thought about it. I remember my parents would say that we were invited to this or that relative's wedding. So you just knew that one day you would be getting married too. You could not say that you were not getting married because you knew you would be. Nana was a very good person. He was the most kind and caring person. Some girls were not so lucky. They got husbands who drank a lot and beat them.

After we got married, we went to Nana's parents' house where we would be living. I spent my first night there sleeping with my mother-in-law and sister-in-law. The next day I was taken back home by my brother, who came for me. There I stayed for one week. Now we had to invite your Nana over to take me back to his home, and we would have to give him a dowry. But he sent his brother instead, so we did not have to give a dowry. I went to live with my in-laws. There I cooked and cleaned for them. Nana earned seventy-five cents per day when we got married. Together your Nana and I worked our land planting and harvesting rice. We would have to travel four to five miles to get to it. We usually stopped halfway to rest. We would make a camp and catch fish and cook. Our work was hard and we did it alone. We sowed the seeds, then transplanted the seedlings, then cut the rice stalks, then thrashed them by walking the cows on them. Sometimes we had two or three cows. We then bagged the rice and put it onto a little boat alongside the banks we have to pull ourselves by hand. This is a long way, 4 to 5 miles. Then we took the rice to the mill where we soaked, dried and milled it. I wish your Nana was alive today. He would be having such an easy and enjoyable life. [I then noticed for the first time that she was still wearing her wedding ring.] When your Nana and I got married, we did not have a marriage certificate. The British did not issue them when you got married young. But people still got married with a wedding ceremony. During my time, daughters-in-law were required to have a tattoo on their right hand; otherwise, their in-laws would not take anything from them to eat. My in-laws did not make me get one, but I decided to do it since I knew the custom. But if I had known how much it hurt I would have chosen a much smaller one. Also, mothers did not take any food from their married daughters unless they paid for it. My mother-in-law would take food and water with her when she went visiting her daughter. She would not stay more than a day. Mothers could do anything at their son's house, though. My explanation for this, from what I know, is that a son retains the family's name whereas the daughter takes on the name of her husband. The daughter becomes an outsider of some sort. The son does the parents' funeral services but not the daughter.

Comments:

When I first heard that I had to do an interview with a grandparent, I rejected the idea completely. I said to myself, "Oh, no! Please, of all things, not this!" The only grandparent available was my grandmother. I said to myself, "Why did I not have to do this when my grandfather was alive?" He was a fantastic person whom I would have enjoyed interviewing. I never had that impression of my grandmother. All I felt for her was not so nice emotions. She is a Scorpio like myself. And being a Scorpio, I know them well. I have always seen the dark side of her, which is not very nice. But she also has a soft side to her. This I realize as I am writing. I never thought about this before. I somehow knew deep inside me that this interview would definitely change my feelings, as it of course did. I had tried being objective but could not maintain it while sitting across from her and listening to her. She did a lot of hurtful and mean things to my family. This interview has resurfaced a lot of painful memories for me. Now that I have done the interview, I have mixed feelings. Part of me says to give her a chance and the other part says not to. Should I forget and forgive? Should I get to know the other side of her before it is too late? My feelings are confused. All I know is that I feel like letting go, but I am hesitant. This has been a very worthwhile experience for me. I have learned a lot by doing this assignment. I have found out a lot of things, personal and impersonal, which I would not have otherwise known.

nadia latchoo

the second and only daughter among three children, Safiran Nadir, my maternal grandmother, was born on June 11, 1923, to Jainab and Mohammed Nadir, who were very young parents in the suburbs of British Guiana.

Safiran was born and grew up in a one-story, shingle-framed house which was elevated about ten feet off the ground. It had, besides a tiny kitchen, one bedroom and a living room which became very crammed after the birth of her second brother. However, the narrowness of the rooms was compensated for in good weather by open doors and open windows and a very big yard. This was possible because Guyana, then British Guiana, is a tropical country.

My grandmother's father, Mohammed Nadir, was, as was customary, the head of the home and the main bread-winner. He worked on the sugar plantation as a laborer and was later promoted to a driver (he supervised other field workers). It should be noted that his parents were brought to British Guiana from India to work on these very sugar estates as indentured laborers. My grandmother's mother, Jainab, was described as an ideal mother and housewife, "the first to rise and the last to go to bed," eating only when time permitted. This trait, no doubt, has been emulated by my grandmother because to this day, even though she is 73, she takes care of her married children and grandchildren. Jainab, besides taking care of her children in all respects, physically and morally, planted a vegetable garden, reared chickens and took care of the cattle.

Safiran, my grandmother, was not given the opportunity to go to school. She told me that the school was very far from where they lived and in those days parents did not think it was necessary to educate girl children. She therefore shared some of the household responsibilities from a very tender age. At age 11, she was already cooking on a fire-side (mud-stove) and was washing clothes. This was done by the side of a trench where she had to rub soap on the garments and then use a beater (a short, flat bat) to beat the clothes, then wash them in the trench. The clothes were then put on lines to dry. She also helped to care for her brothers. She remembered doing dishes using soap and ashes from the fire-side. The ashes helped to make the dishes and pots shine. She also dabbed under the house using wet mud (a mixture of clay and cow's down). This made under the house look very clean and smooth.

Drinking water was not available in individual homes, so when it did not rain she had to carry pails on her head and walk maybe about a mile to the nearest well-pipes. She also recalled going on her knees and scrubbing the green-heart floor with a scraper to make the boards red and smooth. As grandma discussed her chores as a young child, she sighed and said, "You children today are so lucky, you don't have to worry about blowing a fire or getting your knees all bruised and darkened. Everything is different now, gas stoves, washing machines, polished floors...." (At this point, I thought what a hard life to have at such a young age.)

My grandmother grew up as a Muslim who believed in Islam. She did not go to mosque, but her brothers and father went every Friday. She observed the religion by praying at

home with her mother. Her parents were very strict. She had
no friends and was never allowed to go to parties or functions. She had to dress very modestly at all times and keep
herself very clean despite her old clothes. She was not allowed to be seen eating on the street or speaking loudly. She
had to always be respectful to grown–ups or peers. She
addressed everyone as uncle, aunt, brother or sister. She
remembered that anyone who saw a child misbehaving had
the authority to spank him or her. Her family could not have
their dinner until the sun was set and the lamp was lit, (they
had no electricity).

Asked if she enjoyed anything in her early childhood,
she recalled a favorite doll she got one Christmas after her
parents took her to the city, Georgetown. She saw the doll in
a store and cried bitterly until her mother bought it for her.
She said her mother used to make her cloth dolls, but when
she got this special doll she started to sew little bonnets and
dresses for her. She also had furniture and tea sets made out
of clay and she enjoyed playing doll house by herself.
"Sometimes my parents took me to the cinema to see Indian
movies but that was very rare," she said.

Their meals consisted of vegetables they grew in their
backyard, fish caught from the nearby trenches and chickens
and ducks they reared. They also got lots of milk from the cows
and goats they had. They planted rice, a main diet for them.

When she was sick, her parents used mainly herbal
medicines. For example, fever–grass tea for fevers, cow-foot
leaf or castor oil leaf for headaches, dye mixed with ground
onions for sprains and white leery for stomach pains. Aloe
was used for cuts and bruises. In severe cases the family
would go to the local doctor who was miles away.

Not only were her parents very strict, but from what she
told me, I don't think they knew how to be affectionate.
Most of the time they would be very serious. She recalled

not being allowed to join in conversations carried on by her parents or grown–ups even when they involved her. She was not allowed to argue or refuse any request or orders made by any member of the family. Obedience was very important and callous behavior was unheard of. On Fridays her father got paid and she smiled as she recalled him bringing home a paper bag full of candy. He gave each of the children a six-pence piece. They each had a savings box made from a sardine tin with a little slit at the top and it was nailed on the wall in a secure corner. "My younger brother sometimes used to take a pointer broom, stick a sticky paste on it and steal my savings. I cried when this happened."

In those times, girls were not allowed to have boy-friends. They were expected to be very chaste virgins at the time of marriage. If they were not found pure on their wed-ding night, they were sent back to their parents' home and that was considered a disgrace to the entire family. Mar-riages were arranged. At age 16, my grandmother recalled she was dressed in her prettiest frock and taken to her uncle's house. "I did not know why I was taken there and I could not have asked any questions. My mother and aunt took me into a bedroom and put a shawl over my head, covering my face." They later took her out into the living room. Sitting there were her father, uncle and a strange young man who she later learned was to be her future hus-band. She recalls never looking up at him once, but as he was leaving she took a peek at him. Asked what she thought of her betrothed, she replied, "I thought his nose was too big but other than that I just knew that I had no other choice." Her uncle knew this young man and he arranged the mar-riage. From conversations between her parents, she learned that his name was Ziro Deen and that he was 26 years old. She never saw him after that first meeting until eight months later on her wedding day.

Preparations began months ahead for the wedding ceremony. Many relatives and friends were invited. The wedding took place on a beautiful August Sunday in 1940. The wedding ceremony was in the yard under a very large tarpaulin tent. It was done in Muslim rites. "My parents killed one cow and six sheep for the occasion. Everyone who attended the wedding was well fed but there was no alcohol." The ceremony consisted of among other things the repetition of matrimonial vows and the handing over of the gifts brought by the groom. Gifts from the groom included the wedding dress and ornaments to be worn on that day. Gifts also included the Mohar, a dowry that is given after the bride tells the groom how much she would like. It could be cash or jewelry. At the end of the ceremony, gifts including cows, sheep, cash and jewelry were given to the newlyweds.

At this point she remembered feeling sad and scared. The thought of leaving home and her parents to go to an entirely new environment with a stranger made her nervous.

After the wedding proceedings the groom and his wedding party left with her and her companion for the groom's home. It is traditional that the bride takes a chaperone who never leaves her side and has to remain with her throughout the wedding night. She remembered feeling shy, but everyone there did their best to make her comfortable. The next day she returned to her parents' home, as was customary, and the following Sunday her husband returned for her and all her belongings.

This was the beginning of a new stage in her life. Gradually she adjusted and tried to practice the teachings and advice of her parents and adult relatives. Her husband was patient and it helped. Three months after marriage she conceived but unfortunately she had a miscarriage. One year later she gave birth to her first child, a son, and had ten other children who were one year to fifteen months apart. She proudly said, "I feel so happy to have all my children and grandchildren around me." Unfortunately her last son passed away a few years ago, leaving her with ten children, six daughters and four sons. The eldest was 55 years old and the youngest 36. She also enjoys thirty-two grandchildren and twenty-one great-grandchildren. Grandma said she never worked outside the home, but she remembered having babies to care for every day and hardly had time for a rest. Like her mother, she sometimes forgot her own meal times, "But today it is rewarding to sit back and reap the fruit of my sacrifices, ten beautiful children who have kept my head up." (When asked if she enjoyed sex or just participated because her husband wanted to, she laughed and didn't answer.)

Ten years ago my grandparents migrated to the United States when they were sponsored by their youngest daughter. My grandma, as I mentioned earlier, is now 73, and my grandpa is 83. They still reside with their youngest daughter in the Bronx. My grandma is still active around the home despite her pains. Asked if she had any regrets in life, she paused and answered, "I am really sorry that I never went to school." She continued that that was one reason why she made sure that all of her children had a sound education. Among her ten children, she raised three teachers, one insurance manager, a mechanic, an upholsterer, two seamstresses, a designer and a housewife.

Grandma feels that children in the United States have too much freedom. She doesn't like the idea that they watch so much television, the way some of them dress for school and the way they disrespect adults. She admits, though, that this country has lots of opportunities to grow.

My grandparents are still happily living together after fifty-six years of marriage. They enjoy sitting and talking about their earlier years, although sometimes they end up arguing.

As I compare my early childhood and teenage years with my grandmother's, I realize that my generation is indeed fortunate for the choices we have. And I can't help feeling that my grandmother was deprived of her childhood and youth. I hope that one day I will be able to tell my grandchildren about the way I was brought up just the way my grandmother told me how she was brought up.

nga wah (alice) chau

my grandmother, Chang Chui Ya, was born on December 28, 1898, in Shanghai, China. She was born into a wealthy family. She was the kindest, most understanding, and most forgiving woman that I have ever met. I asked her what were the most memorable events of her life. She said there were three stages in her life: marriage, family and struggling to survive during the Sino-Japanese War.

My grandmother's grandfather had worked with the last emperor. Her parents wanted to arrange her marriage. However, she hated the idea of an arranged marriage and told her parents that it was an old- fashioned tradition. She said, "If I wanted to be married, I must have a person that I love." However, her parents persuaded her and invited a woman called a matchmaker to come to their house. The matchmaker brought a painting of her future husband to her parents and exchanged it for a painting of my grandmother. The couple did not meet until the day of the wedding, when my grandmother was 16 years old. I asked her, "How did you travel?" She said, "At that time, there was no car or wagon at all. The only transportation was the Chinese hand-held wagon. This wagon was carried by four persons while one person sat inside." The party was full of people. She was in the bedroom where she was sitting on the bed with a red handkerchief covering her head. The bed curtain was made of red silk. The blanket was sewn with the design of a pair of dragons. My grandmother continued, "I was so nervous. I held my handkerchief very tightly. Finally, there was a man who came into the bedroom who was your grandfather. He sat down on the bed. He waited for a long time to take off the handkerchief because he was so nervous, until his mother came to the bedroom." She asked him, "Why didn't you take off the bride's handkerchief?" He said, "Mom, I was afraid." His mother said, "Let me take a look at the bride. Wow! She is beautiful." He then finally took off the handkerchief. That was the first time I saw his real face without looking at the painting." I asked my grandmother, "Grandmom, didn't you feel funny or uncomfortable at that time?" She said, "Actually, I felt very uncomfortable talking to your grandfather because it was the first time that we met. I had so many questions in my mind such as what were his interests. When he started to talk to me, we found out we somehow had common interests. That's why we got along so well." I told my grandmother that she was a very lucky lady.

Her family was one of the happiest memories of her life. She enjoyed being a member of an extended family that lived with my great-grandparents in one house. She remembered that before she was married her mother taught her how to respect her future parents-in-law and follow their wishes. She got along well with everyone in the house.

I asked her, "Is it true that the son is more important than the daughter?" She said, "True, because the sons carried their families' last name and families' business to the future." Then she told me what happened during her first pregnancy. Actually, she did not know what happened to her. All she felt was something moving inside of her body and she was dizzy and vomiting all of the time. She told her mother-in-law, who found a doctor. In those days, the doctor didn't use an instrument to hear your pulse. He asked her to lie down on the bed and took her hand in his. Then he put his two fingers on top of her wrist to hear her pulse. That's how he determined her condition. The doctor told her that she was pregnant. When her family heard the news, they were very happy—especially her in-laws. They both wanted to have as many children in the family as possible.

A few months later, she gave birth to her first child, my first uncle, Yai Chang Chow. I asked her, "Did the doctor help you?" She said, "At that time, there were no doctors to help deliver babies. All they had were midwives who came to the bedroom and helped mothers give birth." Her mother-in-law was very happy because the child was a son. Twelve years later, another child was born, my second uncle, Loon Chang Chow. My grandmother said, "Your first and second uncles were both born in the year of the dragon. That was why your grandfather chose the character of dragon for their names." In the year of the second birth both her parents-in-law passed away.

Her husband opened a clothing materials store in the city. In 1927, communism took over China. In 1929, her third son, my father, Man Lung Chau was born. Later, two more children were born, but both died of measles a month later. I asked her, "Was there no cure?" She said, "There was no cure then for this disease. Somehow, I felt lonely because I had lost two children in the same month." Time went by so fast, her husband always kept her company and his business was doing so well. In 1933, she gave birth to her fourth son, Ngan Lung Chau. She told me that he always did what he pleased. I asked her, "Do your sons have anything in common?" She said, "Yes, they have one common quality, stubbornness. They got it from your grandfather." Anyway, they were good kids.

In 1935, her fifth child was born and it was a daughter. Sons and daughters were just starting to be treated equally. When I asked her what she meant by equal, she replied, "As I mentioned before, boys were treated like treasure. Many people thought that it was wrong—as they thought there were some things girls could do better than boys. For example, girls can help their mothers do housework and take good care of them." I said to her, "It's about time that girls have the same status as boys."

My grandmother could not forget what happened during the Sino-Japanese War when the Japanese took over China on July 7, 1937. That was the most horrifying experience for her family. Her husband became ill and passed on a few days later. Her four young children were at a tender age and needed a lot of attention, but her oldest son was about 25 years old and was ready to be married. Her second son found a job as a sailor traveling out of the country. My father went out selling cigarettes on a city street, and my grandmother joined him every day. Her fourth son was in school. She also told me that the Japanese then prohibited Chinese people from selling their merchandise on the streets. At the time, her third son was 11 years old and had to go to work as a sailor like his middle brother. While they both were out of the country, they sent money home to support the family.

Finally, my grandmother moved to the United States and lived with my family. She was amazed by the number of cars on the streets and was uncomfortable with the different environment. She decided to return to China. Before she left the U.S., I asked her, "What do you think about your life? Is it worthy?" She said, "I think it's worthy to see my children grow up and they are good kids. Therefore, I'm very happy they are the way they are."

eliзaвeth watts

I approached the interview with my grandfather with some trepidation, as he has always been what I would kindly describe as a reticent man. I arrived at my grandparent's apartment in Bensonhurst, Brooklyn, with butterflies in my stomach and a sense that I was not going to get much out of my grandfather. To my surprise he greeted me enthusiastically and seemed oddly disappointed when I explained that all this was for a school project and not out of personal interest.

My grandfather, James Aloysius Wallace, was born the oldest of eleven children, only seven of whom lived to adulthood, at home in Youngstown, Ohio, on January 1, 1914. His parents were immigrants, his mother, Rose, from Ireland and his father, Robert, from Scotland. My grandfather doesn't remember much of Ohio, which the family left after the death of his next-born sibling, Mary Catherine, when she was 3 years old. James was 4 when they moved to Brooklyn.

The family, which now consisted of Rose, Robert, James and his younger brothers Paul and Sean, moved into a small house on Conover Street in the Red Hook section of Brooklyn. The house was situated behind the larger house of Rose's sister Mary Margaret and her husband, Michael Murphy.

James's father, Robert, had not wanted to move from Ohio, particularly not into a small house in Brooklyn which did not even face the street but the back of the Murphys', from whom they were renting the house. Rose, however, could not stay in Youngstown after the death of Mary Catherine and did seem much happier after the move.

So it was here, in the "back house" on Conover Street, that my grandfather grew up. It was here he learned to play Gaelic football from his father and to sing all the old Irish tunes from his mother. Personally, he thought all of this to be nonsense and a waste of time, but his brother and, later, more sisters played the games and sang with relish and seemed to look forward to these family activities. So he said nothing and joined in when he could not make up any excuses to get out of it.

Life was neither hard nor easy for James, it just was what it was, and from the earliest age he learned to do what was expected of him without complaint and largely without joy.

By the standards of the day the Wallaces were neither rich nor poor; even during the depression years Robert found steady work down at the Brooklyn shipyards. He was a strong man, a workhorse, and was not known to drink his wages of a Friday night, as was the curse of many of his contemporaries. Rose helped out by bringing in washing and ironing from the families who could afford to send it out, and from the youngest age, James could be seen running errands or delivering newspapers and groceries.

Life went on for the Wallaces and for James in a steady, even fashion. Even with the subsequent births (and a few deaths) of more siblings and countless cousins in front at the Murphys', James was never seen to cry and very rarely to laugh. He was adequate in his studies and neither failed nor excelled. He was usually described by his teachers as taciturn but no trouble. Some of them said they barely even noticed he was in the room at all.

At Mass, it was much the same. While all of his brothers and male cousins served as altar boys at St. Michael's at one time or another, James never did. Yet he never missed a Sunday Mass and could often be seen in the evenings on his front porch praying the Rosary with Rose's pale blue beads. His brothers mocked him, calling him Father Wallace. Rose often referred to him as the old man.

It seemed the only person James had much time for was his uncle, Big Mike Murphy. Everyone thought it strange they should get on so well since they were, temperamentally, polar opposites. Michael Murphy was a big booming man, always ready with a story or a joke, and no one in the family understood the attraction. Big Mike knew it was, in part, envy. James wished he could be more like Mike Murphy, but just did not know how. But beyond that there was a genuine friendship and an affection for each other. Mike just wished he knew how to draw James out more.

After an uneventful life in high school, James went on to complete an equally uneventful stint at college. He then took a job as an assistant bookkeeper at Brach's, a candy company where two of his sisters, Patricia and Susan, were already working in the assembly lines, packaging chocolates. He was 22 and the year was 1936. He was good at his work, very steady and never out a day sick, so he rose in the company and in two years became a senior bookkeeper. He earned a fair living with which he helped support his family, with whom he was still living, and started a savings account which grew steadily.

It was in 1938 that things changed dramatically for James, for it was then that the McKennas arrived in Red Hook. The McKenna clan moved to Red Hook from Chicago, where, or so the neighborhood gossips claimed, there had been some scandal involving Mrs. McKenna and one of her sons' high school friends. The men of Red Hook believed this story as Mrs. McKenna, for all of her nine children, was a stunning woman. She had long, flowing ginger hair as did all of her five daughters, right down to the baby Sarah, who was just born and there was some speculation as to who exactly had fathered the child.

At any rate, the men (eligible and otherwise) of Red Hook were entranced by the McKenna woman. They were bathing more often, dressing better and old man Green down at Green's Pharmacy on Pineapple Street said he'd never seen such a run on Brylcream in his life. He couldn't keep the shelves stocked with it.

The only exception to this madness, of course, was James. He couldn't stand to see his brothers and cousins acting like a bunch of fools over a group of redheaded sisters. That is, until the day he first laid eyes on Maura McKenna, at nine o'clock Mass at St. Michael's Church on Sunday, September 22, 1938. Contrary to his nature, he fell in love with her at first sight and vowed to himself and to his God that he would do all in his power to win her.

Much to everyone's surprise (including his own), win her he did, and the whole neighborhood turned out when James Aloysius Wallace, then age 25, wed Maura Anne Teresa McKenna, age 20, on June 14, 1939. The reception afterwards at the Murphys' house on Conover Street was a huge event, and everyone said they had never seen a change the likes of which Maura had brought about in James. He was laughing and dancing and had even gotten up to sing one of his mother's favorite old Irish tunes. No one was more thrilled than Michael Murphy at the changes in James since he'd first met Maura.

James was deliriously happy for the next three years. Maura bore him two daughters in quick succession, Rose in 1940 and Michaela, my mother, who was named for Michael Murphy, in 1941. He doted on them and on his beloved Maura. But his happiness was to be short-lived.

On a bitter cold day in the winter of 1941, James came home from work to the lovely small house on Richards Street he had bought as a wedding gift for Maura and found his world shattered. The house was dark and cold, his daughters were hungry, shivering and wailing loudly, and Maura was gone. A short, terse note stated she had fallen in love and run off with Enzo Aghuili, a young Italian immigrant known in the neighborhood for his expensive clothing, fast cars and even faster women and a purported family connection to organized crime.

It was this tragedy that broke my grandfather's spirit, but he carried on for the girls' sake. All of his sisters and most of his sisters–in–law offered to take the girls and raise them with their own children, but James refused: they were his children and he'd raise them.

Being the sole support of his two daughters, he was exempt from service when the U.S. entered World War II. He did, however, lose his favorite brother, Sean. Big Mike Murphy lost his oldest son, Michael Jr., and that was the beginning of the end for James' cherished uncle. Although he lived another five years, his spirit died with his oldest son.

James only heard from Maura once after that, in early 1942, in the form of divorce papers, which he signed without fuss. The papers gave him sole custody of Rose and Michaela.

In 1945, he married Angela Finch, a neighborhood schoolteacher and the woman I always believed was my biological grandmother, at City Hall, without any of the fanfare that had accompanied his first wedding. She was a quiet, plain woman and she raised James' daughters as her own. And though she never bore him any children, she was content with Rose and Michaela and considered herself a good mother. So did James and he left the raising of the girls to Angela after that.

There were only a few things that James insisted on with his girls. One was that they attend Mass every Sunday and every Holy Day of Obligation without exception, and the other was an inordinate strictness with the girls over friends, particularly those of the opposite sex. He was very concerned that they comport themselves in a manner that he considered appropriate for young women. He did not want them talking or laughing too loudly in public or in any other manner drawing attention to themselves. In other words, he did not want them behaving like their real mother. He would never have put it that way, of course. Not even to himself.

Despite this, he was a good husband and father. He worked at Brach's until his retirement in 1980, eventually reaching the position of vice president of accounting. He moved his family to a modest home in Bay Ridge, Brooklyn, and sent his daughters to Our Lady of Perpetual Help Catholic School and then to Brooklyn College.

After his daughters were married and gone he sold the house in Bay Ridge and bought a one-bedroom condominium in Bensonhurst, where he and Angela still live.

I have gained a new respect for my grandfather through this interview, and from my grandfather I now have a clearer understanding of the old expression "still waters run deep." He told me he is still a happy man, with no regrets, for in his lifetime he has experienced both great passion and a steady, loving companionship, and although both were not experienced with the same woman, it's more than any man could ask for.

For my part, I don't think I'll wait for another school project to sit and talk with my grandfather again.

JEFFREY LEE

my grandmother is probably one of the most caring and loving people I have ever known. She died about eight years ago from a combination of old age and mental illness. At that time, she was about 85 years old. During her lifetime, she had managed to raise three sons and live through some major wars (World War II and the Vietnam War). She is my father's mother, and she loved me from the day I was born till the day she died. She probably loved me more than her own children or anyone else in the world. Here are my recollections of my grandmother:

When I was really young, about 3 or 4 years old, I remember my grandmother baby-sitting me during the daytime because my parents were not home. My father had to work the day shift in a restaurant, and my mother was visiting her relatives in Taiwan. I remember my grandmother playing with me, talking to me, always telling me to be a good boy and grow up to become to a good young man. She would make homemade soup for me and tell me that it was good for my health. I would always gulp the soup with eagerness because it made me happy to see my grandmother happy. She cared for me as if she were my mother, and I loved her for that when I was young.

However, things changed when my mother came back from Taiwan. My mother was pretty upset when she heard that my grandmother had been baby-sitting when she was gone (obviously mother did not like her). Then my mother started telling me that my grandmother was an evil woman who was trying to poison me with the food she fed me. She told me not to mention this to my father or else he would beat me up for being a bad boy. All this did not make sense to me at the time, but I listened to my mother anyway since she was my parental figure and I was taught to listen to my elders. After a period of time, I really did think that my grandmother was trying to harm me. I avoided eating the food she would personally make for me, fearing that I would get sick from eating it. I avoided her touching me, fearing that her touch would wither my skin. I feared going inside her apartment since I had nightmares that cockroaches would jump on me and eat me alive. Basically, I was afraid of my grandmother and I wanted nothing to do with her.

My mother's influence would continue strongly into my grade school years. By then, my grandmother's health had deteriorated so badly that she was sick all the time. She would also have mental lapses at times, forgetting where she was while walking the streets. One day, my father brought her to our apartment saying that she would be staying in our home for a while. I remember her telling me to go to her so that she could have a good look at me, but I was afraid. I was afraid that whatever disease she had she would give to me. I think it really broke her heart that I was afraid of her, and that really made me feel bad. One time I remember my father telling me that one night when I wasn't home, my grandmother went out into the cold to look for me. She called for me and couldn't find me. The scary thing was that no one knew where she was and everybody went out look-ing for her. When they found her, she was crying and mumbling that Fai-Fai (my Chinese name) didn't love her any more. That really broke my heart, and I was beginning to doubt what my mother said about my grandmother. Then one day, when I was in school, my mother decided to blast the radio to the max when my grandmother was sleeping. That somehow drove my grandmother "crazy" and she was moved to the hospital that day. I hated my mother from that day onward. That was also the last time I saw my grandmother alive. She died a couple of months later.

It was during the summer of 1990 that my grandmother had died. The news of her death didn't really hit until I went to the funeral home and saw her peaceful, wrinkled body in the casket. I guess I couldn't believe that she was dead because she had been there for me ever since I could remember. Her death hit my family members really hard. All the members, with the exception of my sister, my mother and me, were grieving over her death. Even the in-laws who attended the funeral cried. At the time, I didn't understand why they were crying so much. But then one of my in-laws whom I was close to came up to me and said something that I will always remember. "Why aren't you crying? Huh? You know that she LOVED YOU VERY MUCH!" Those words and the way my in-law said them woke me up from a nasty reality: I am not a good person. That day, I had a couple of revelations: one, I realized I was a horrible grandson. I never showed the respect and love to her that she had shown to me. She gave me gifts and money, and I took them for granted. Worst of all, I took my grandmother love for me for granted. My second revelation was that I realized how much I hated my mother that day. Ever since that day, I have hated and distrusted her for her lies.

During the three days of the funeral, I never did cry once. Looking back, I still don't know why I never cried. There was a good lesson I learned from those days of sadness. That lesson was that my mother is a heartless, #!*%!@# bitch (excuse my language). She had the nerve to make fun of the people who were crying out of sadness, saying that they were idiots for crying over a person who should have been dead long ago.

Nowadays, I don't hear my family mention my grandmother that much. (Only one exception: when my mother uses her name saying that I should be joining her because I am as worthless as she. I am usually tempted to slap my mother across the face but, out of respect for my elders, I haven't.) During my freshman year of high school, I would go on special Sundays, with my father and my uncles, to pay respect to her and my grandfather in the afterlife. As time went on, I couldn't go because of the amount of schoolwork I had to do. I haven't gone to their graveyards since my sophomore year of high school.

While writing this paper, I came to realize how much my grandmother affected the course of my life, how much I learned from her. I learned how to help others, kindness, hope, and the most important one of all, love. She taught me how to love another human being and I will never forget that. God bless you, Grandma, and I wish you a better life in the afterlife than your last years on earth.

ka woo lok

this interview with my grandparent was very interesting. My grandmother told me a lot about her life and my grandfather. My grandmother told me how difficult life was back in China. My grandmother was born during the 1920s. She lived with her parents in a tiny house in the countryside.

When she was young she could not go to school because she was poor and because she was a girl, and as a girl she was supposed to stay home and help her mother with the house chores. The boys went to school but not beyond the fourth grade. The boys did not finish their education because they had to help their father farm and earn a living.

My grandmother and grandfather never saw each other before they were married. Their marriage was a blind marriage, a marriage set up by both their parents. They did not get married because of love but for procreation. After they were married, my grandmother moved in with my grandfather. She had to take care of her in-laws and her own parents and she had to do all the cleaning for both sides of the family. She did laundry for a living. She did not have a washing machine but did the laundry by the river bank with a baby on her back. She took care of neighbors' children and did house chores just to help support her family. My grandfather

was a fisherman. He helped catch fish for people, and whatever fish were left he took home for dinner.

A year or so after their first child they saved enough
money and moved to Hong Kong. Life was still difficult. My
grandfather found a job making egg rolls. Since my grandmother had no experience in working besides house chores,
she stayed home taking care of her children. She has seven
children, three boys and four girls. They stayed in Hong
Kong for a few years, then had enough money to move to
the United States. She found a job working in a factory in
Chinatown in New York. Their oldest son, my father, quit
school at the fourth grade to help support the family and
help support my uncles and aunts through school.

Now my grandfather is dead because he and my grandmother had a huge argument and he left and went to Hong
Kong. The environment did not suit him and he died in the
hospital. After all those years of working he contracted a lot
of illnesses. My grandmother never felt so guilty in her life.
She was crying throughout this interview. She is now a
lonely widow living in Boston. She deserves this punishment. I never did like my grandmother because she never
liked my family.

LAURIE BARBERIE

O n a Monday night in November 1919, the 24th to be exact, a beautiful baby boy was born in a two-family house on Usher Avenue in Bristol, Rhode Island, the smallest state in the union.

Orsola and Frank Zesare were immigrants who traveled long and hard from Italy to reach their long-awaited goal: to become American citizens. This dream did come true for Orsola, Frank and their son Antonio and they soon became the Zesare family on Bradford Street.

Eight years later, the baby was now a young boy. Antonio Joseph Zesare attended third grade at St. Carmel Parish in Bristol. His family being practicing Catholics, Antonio served as an altar boy in church during these years. Throughout his childhood, he enjoyed playing football, horseshoes and stickball in the streets of Bristol. He often got on his one-dollar boxing gloves, bought at the Five and Dime, and "beat the hell out of his cousin because he was a sorehead."

At the ripe old age of 12, Anthony and his family moved to a three-family house on Jefferson Street in Bushwick, Brooklyn. The Zesares did not live there for long. "If a I'm not mistaken...a the next address was a...89 Central Avenue." This house was only down the block from the last. Anthony went to junior high at P.S. 145 and then it was off to high school.

During the summer before high school, Tony moved once again, to 43 Skillman Avenue in Williamsburg, Brooklyn. As I sit here writing this, my grandmother, sitting beside me interjects, "Jesus babe, how many times did you put the god damn ii-lo li-num down! I been in my one house forty years. It's da trudce!" I can't help but laugh at them arguing.

For two years, Tony traveled back and forth to Greenpoint to attend, as he says it "Eeestin Districk High School." Once again my grandmother speaks her mind because my grandfather has got up to get himself a sugarfree fudge pop. "Yeah babe, and ya fatha, when you was in high school, ya fatha be waitin fa you in da rain wit an umbrella and galoshes!" "Well babe, wudda ya gonna do, dat's my fatha!"

After completing two years of high school, he quickly went to work. President FDR passed the WPA (Works Progress Administration) bill. It created jobs for many unemployed. This was to help get many families, including Tony's, off "home relief," today called welfare. Under the WPA, Tony worked backbreaking hours digging ditches for contractors in Brooklyn. He quit that job real soon!

"GREETINGS, YOU'RE IN THE ARMY NOW," read the letter received by 23-year-old Anthony Zesare on a cold January day in 1943. With no further thought, Anthony knew he was now a soldier.

Tony had orientation at Fort Dix, New Jersey. "From there they shipped me out to Pennsylvania. And then we stood there for a couple a weeks… a then we got on the train and we were headed for Ft. Leonard Wood, Missouri, where I took my three months' training for a about two weeks… and a then they shipped us out again to VOIR-GIN-YA.

That's where da 'Banana Boat' wuz. That would take you across da seas…and a…I landed in North Africa…" "Yeah dats where da CANNONBALLS were, right babe," interrupted my grandmother in an attempt to say 'cannibals.'

"Babe, why you call them cannonballs, those A-RABS, they stole my barracks bag!" "Uh, Laurie, grams, they had no TUR-LITS in Africa, no flushbowls YEESAGO! It the trudce, Laurie," my grandmother exclaimed. After three and a half years of service, Tony received a purple heart. He was honorably discharged and belonged to the 52–club. This enabled him to receive twenty dollars a week for 52 weeks. When the weeks were up, poor, lonely Tony was looking for a job. But little did he know he would find a little more than a job. April 19, 1948, was a big day for Laura Santillo. She got up early for a job interview and then planned on buying shoes. She started her day by arriving at the unemployment agency on Schermerhorn Street at 9 o'clock in the morning.

"I was sitting on a bench and a all of a sudden, this stranger approached me. He had a newspaper unda his arm and a beige jacket on. He sat next to me (the only person in the place, leaving every other bench available). He asked me how long I was sittin there. I told him I was waiting since nine o'clock. With no further words, I went up to the desk for my interview. When I was finished he passed by me, as it was his turn for the interview. Feeling sorry because I did not get the job, I was waiting outside for him. I was curious to find out if he got a job. He came outside and asked me if I knew how to get to Cherry Street. I told him we outta getta policeman to help us. Now…knowing the directions…this stranger ova here, he asked me if I would like to get a cuppa coffee. I knew I had to go buy shoes but I decided to go with him anyway. We went to the soda shop, down the basement and sat there. He asked me if I wanted a slice a' pie. I asked him, "Ainchya gonna have a piece a pie?" He simply replied, "no." "A year later, I find out that Tony Zesare only had 35 cents in his pocket that day and he spent it on a piece a pie for me."

Forty-nine years, two children, and one granddaughter later, the two strangers, one looking for a job, the other looking for shoes, have found a united life together. That day they must have been looking for each other.

Jennifer Salinas

my father's parents were Sephardic Jews born in La Plata, Argentina. When they were married they decided to move to Buenos Aires, Argentina. They had seven boys and two girls. My father, named Robert, is the second-youngest of the boys.

My father grew up on a huge farm. The main house which the family lived in consisted of six bedrooms, one large kitchen, three bathrooms, a playroom, a living room and a dining room. In back of the house there was a pool and there was a house for the help. On the farm there were horses, cows, pigs, goats and chickens.

My dad's mother was a devoted mother. Her children were her top priority. In fact, she never left them with a baby-sitter. She strongly believed in spending all of her time with her children. Her son Robert enjoyed spending quality time with her and helped her to sell the eggs, vegetables and fruit from their farm to local people.

His father was a diplomat who represented Argentina. Most of the time he was sent to different European countries for his diplomatic duties. His father also imported and exported agricultural machinery. Robert, as well as the other children, were not as close to their father as they were to their mother.

As for family activities, my father, Robert, and his family had meals together, went to the stadium to watch soccer (which is called futbol in Argentina), went to the park and to movies. In the summer they vacationed in Italy and Spain. Religion was very important to the family. On Friday evenings the Sabbath candles were lit. A traditional meal was prepared which consisted of challah, chicken and soup with matzo balls and home baked sponge cake. On Saturdays Robert and his family attended Sabbath services at a nearby temple.

Unfortunately, when my Father was 7, his beloved mother passed away. He truly adored her. It was the most traumatic experience of his childhood. In the South American culture a man was taught not to cry. He had to be a macho man. When a man cried he was considered a sissy. He had to learn how to deal with his emotions. The only way he got stronger was to reminisce with his siblings about precious memories of his mother.

Because of this traumatic experience the structure of the family fell apart. After Robert's mother passed away, his father hardly spent any time with his children. To escape problems or pressure he worked longer hours and the children were constantly left with a servant.

It was a sudden surprise for my dad and his siblings when his father married one of the servants. The servant was nice when she was simply a servant. When she married his father, she became a true "wicked stepmother." My dad recalls an incident when he was late for dinner and his stepmother burned his lip with a hot spoon and threw out his dinner. His siblings were mistreated as well. She would lock the food cabinets, punish them and use physical force. My dad said, "She had no heart and she was a very cold person."

When Robert told his father about this abuse, his father turned on him and took his stepmother's side. Robert was deeply hurt by his father. Robert decided to live with his older brother Ramon, who was married. Eventually, the older siblings began to move out of the house. They lived with various aunts and uncles. Once my dad moved out, he never bothered with his father again.

Because of his brother Ramon, he began to take an interest in soccer. After school Robert and his brother would play soccer. In high school he was selected to play soccer around South America. One of the countries he played against was Brazil. Pelé was on the Brazilian team Dosanto, but he wasn't as well known as he is today. Pelé went on to become one of the most famous soccer players.

The father was very cold to his children. However, people from the neighborhood would tell my dad that when his father heard about his son playing professional soccer, he would brag to all his friends.

My dad did not want to pursue soccer as a career. He decided to attend college. He graduated from the University of Buenos Aires with a degree in business administration. He heard from friends who had left South America for the United States. They lived in Chicago. They invited him to come to the United States. He stayed with them for two months. When he arrived in Chicago it was snowing and it was very cold. He was wearing a white linen suit. He found it very hard to adjust to the cold weather. He found a job at Whiskland Factory full-time as a stock person in their warehouse. At night he went to school to improve his English. While he was in Chicago he received a letter from his younger brother, Ricky, who was living in Queens, New York. He told him that he could make more money in New York City. Ricky as well as his sister Maria were the only siblings who came to the United States.

Two months later my dad left Chicago to stay with his brother Ricky, his wife, Joanne, and his daughter Marti. Throughout his stay he worked as a part-time liquor sales-man, and he sold real estate. Today my dad is a used car manager at an auto dealership in Westchester.

On an Easter Sunday, my father and his friend Cesar were walking on Fifth Avenue. He says that he saw a beauti-ful blue-eyed blond woman walking with her friend. He told his friend that he was going to marry that young lady. His friend thought he was crazy. Finally, when he caught up with my mom and her friend Eleanor, he introduced himself. At first, she was scared that a strange man was running after her in the street. He asked her if he could take her, together with her friend Eleanor and his friend Cesar, for a drink at La Fonda Del Sol. From that day on they began dating.

They spent all of their free time together. They went to dinner, movies, Broadway shows, operas and museums. Robert proposed to Helene at her place of employment. He gave her a ring and a watch.

On June 6, 1971, Helene and Robert were married at the Spanish Portuguese Synagogue located at 2 West 70th Street in New York City. The attire was formal. My mother wore a white satin and lace wedding gown trimmed with pearls. My father, wore a black tuxedo with a blue shirt. Rabbi Cardozo, the famous Sephardic rabbi, married them. His brother Ricky was his best man. Ricky's 5-year-old daughter, Marti, was the flower girl. His sister was also at the wedding as well as many of my dad's friends. My mom's parents, brother Leslie and their friends and family attended as well. My mom's parents gave her away. The cocktail reception was held at the St. Moritz Hotel located on Central Park South, in New York City. There was live music. They spent their honeymoon in Florida.

When Robert became a father he decided that he was going to be a better father than his own father. My mom and dad had two daughters, Jennifer and Blair. It was a terrible tragedy for my family and me when my sister, Blair Alyson, passed away because of an allergic reaction to a D.P.T. shot. She was only 2 years old.

She is in our hearts forever. We keep her memory alive by speaking about her often. The loss of Blair was very hard for us. When my dad experienced the loss of his mother at 7 years old, he was not allowed to cry. When he lost his daughter, he let all his emotions come out.

elsie cheng

thursday was the day of the week when I stayed at my grandparents' house. I usually liked staying over there because it meant I could stay up until 10:30 or 11 p.m., and I didn't have to listen to mother's nagging. I was also pleased to spend time with my aunt and grandma. Grandpa was more of a mystery to me because he came back around the time I had to sleep, but there usually was enough time to say hello to him. He was a taxi driver, and to me it sounded like a fun and easy way to make a living. Drive people around all day and then go home. He would come in and say hello to me and grandma and turn on the TV, then holler out: "Bring me my tea, and where is my dinner, a–mu?" in his Chinese dialect. "A–mu" means old woman, but it's an impersonal way to address someone you are not very close to. I never heard him call grandma by her name, nor have I heard grandma call him by his name. Their aloofness seemed to be the result of an arranged marriage, which left them no other choice but each other.

While grandma was reheating grandpa's food, he took out what looked like a twenty-dollar bill and exclaimed, "A–mu, look at this twenty-dollar bill I have, they cheated me!" I took a closer look, but it looked like an ordinary rolled up twenty-dollar bill. I unraveled it and instead of

55

Andrew Jackson, I saw George Washington. The culprit
taped a part of the twenty to a one-dollar bill. My grandpa
found it funny and aggravating at the same time because he
had wasted gas for that prank and lost twenty dollar's
worth of business.

When the food was almost ready, grandpa insisted on
saying "A-mu, hurry up, I am starving." The words "please"
and "thank you" never escaped his mouth, but the orders
kept going. Usually by this time, I couldn't help but say
something to my grandma and encourage her to tell him to
do it himself. Never did he lift a finger to help, even on the
weekends. It made me mad that he never helped and he
always called her A–mu; she's his wife, not his servant. Of
course my grandma brushed it aside and went on with her
chores. When I couldn't take the frustration any more, I went
to sleep.

Those were typical Thursday evenings with my grandparents. At that time, both my parents worked and the other
alternative was for me to stay home alone, so I opted to give
my parents a break on Thursdays. Now I usually visit my
grandparents on Saturdays. One Saturday, when my brother
and sister were occupied with the television, I stumbled
upon some photo albums that were set aside on the dining
room table. I opened one and saw a picture with my great–
grandfather and some other women and young boys I didn't
quite recognize. "Ghon ghon, who are these people?"
("Ghon ghon" means maternal grandfather.) He walks in
with his manly strut and big round belly and peers in at the
picture that I point at. "Oh, that's great-grandpa, and see,
your great-grandma is sitting to his left. This woman to his
right is his other wife." "Wait!," I exclaimed, "you mean he
had two wives!" He looked at me and said, why do you look
so surprised, in China, a man had two wives, if he could
afford it." I realized then that this wasn't something that

history books made up, because it was true. "So who is this little boy?" I asked. "That's me, of course," exclaimed my grandpa. I looked at him and the resemblance was there, except he was much thinner and more muscular back then.

I pointed to a picture of grandpa standing in front of a Chinese laundry shop. He explained that he had worked there when he first came to New York City. He went to adult school during the morning because he only had schooling up to the sixth grade, which was two more years than my grandma had. He told me that it was not so tough because he was used to going to school in the mornings in China and then working in the rice fields until late in the evening. So he kept attending the adult classes, which were conducted in his native dialect, for the next four years, until great-grandpa bought a grocery store in Chinatown It was a Chinese-American grocery store, which helped him learn English because he had to speak to the salesmen. "So what happened to the grocery store, ghon ghon?" I asked. "Well, great–grandpa passed away and my brothers and cousins and nephews were getting too old to manage it, so we sold it," he replied.

Since then, grandpa drove a taxicab for the next eighteen years before he retired. After flipping through all those pictures I realized how tough it must have been to drive a taxicab in New York City all day long and then come home and have your granddaughter telling you that you're lazy. I understand now that my grandpa is not the meanest and most uncaring person in the world, but a very hard worker who did what he could to survive in a foreign country.

Whenever I go over to my grandparents' house now, I see how much my grandpa has changed since his retirement. He bakes cupcakes for us when he knows that we are going there, he irons everyone's clothes including whatever of my parents, my uncle and my aunt needs ironing, he actually washes dishes, he goes to the supermarket with my grandma, helps her cook and clean and has even chipped in with grandma's garden. I once thought that he was not capable of doing these things, that he was forever relying on my grandma to do everything for him. All along, what I should have seen was the twelve-hour workdays he used to have and his reluctance to do anything but relax when he came home. Grandma has since learned the art of rebuttal and grandpa's mean, sarcastic remarks are nothing more than jokes turned against him.

I think he is finally getting what he deserves after living a hard life in China, barely scraping by, wondering if the next meal would feed everyone in the family. Now he can finally enjoy life and everything he worked for, a wonderful family and grandchildren to spoil with candy and junk food.

I know that even with only an elementary education, my grandpa knows more than I will ever know, like every short-cut through Manhattan, or all the right ways to iron your shirt or when is the perfect time to harvest bittermelons. I only hope that my grandchildren will find me as admirable as I have found my grandpa to be.

section two
education

I n ancient Greek the word "schole" meant "leisure."
(*Webster's New World Dictionary*, 3d College ed., p. 1201,
Simon and Schuster, New York, 1984). Perhaps this explains the persisting link between school and the leisure
class, and the high illiteracy among the poor. Archeologists
discovered the first school in Sumer (Samuel Noah Kramer,
History Begins in Sumer, Doubleday Anchor, New York, 1959).
The written word created the institution of formal education,
the school, in order to train scribes to keep records, to serve
the palaces and temples.

Paradoxically, the rate of illiteracy in the world increases,
because illiteracy is linked to poverty and high birth rate,
education is linked to high birth control. It is striking how
many grandparents wished they had more education. When
asked, "What regrets do you have?" or "If you had your life
to live again, how would you change it?" almost without
exception they said they wished they had more education.
This is not romanticizing education; it is a practical statement. Research supports their position. Differences in
educational level are by far the most important factor in the
integration and mobility of immigrants, far more important
than immigration policy or labor market structure (*Sociologi-*

cal Abstract, American Sociological Association, 92d Annual
Meeting, p. 93).

In this collection we treat education, a Latin word denot-
ing rearing, bringing up, developing knowledge and skills,
not only in school. Some papers were selected for this chapter because they speak about teaching reading and writing at
home, on the porch, or by a grandmother who reads the
Bible to her family.

We open with a paper about an illiterate grandfather
who is a master storyteller with a deserved reputation and
audience. It is particularly moving that the grandparent
introduces himself as a writer of many books, a magician
who spins stories within stories. His listeners "believe" him.
His fantasy, his reverence and longing for education, are
deeply touching. In this brief paper education assumes a
mythical value; it becomes the ultimate goal worthy of
human endeavor. Somehow, one feels that in its absence
education becomes even more significant. The grandfather is
like a hungry man who in the absence of food is telling
stories. How he wished he were a writer.

"My grandparents were both hard workers who just
wanted to fulfill one thing in life: that was for all ten children to finish school" (Jennifer Sabenano, Manila,
Philippines).

"My grandmother regrets not going to school because
she was and still is a very talented, intelligent and creative
person….She encourages me to study, because she did not
have the same opportunity in her country" (Ana Garcia,
Nicaragua).

"The boys had to dedicate their young lives cultivating
land instead of getting education. My grandfather never
attended school and is therefore illiterate" (Audrey
Gonzales, Dominican Republic).

"Lillian knew there was a better life out there for her and saw education as means to reach those goals" (Yvette Moreno, U.S.A.).

"Her ambition was to have something of her own, something no one could take away from her. It was education" (Diana Cora). In her interview, Ann Foley's grandmother describes the school in a rural village in the south of Ireland: "All the grades, from kindergarten to the last year of high school, were conducted in just one big room with a fireplace at the front. The children were still always frozen....We got a wallop from a bamboo stick...and those were hard wallops too."

Indeed, immigrants' children register higher achievements in high school the less time they and their families have spent in the United States. (*Not Only for Myself*, Martha Minow, The New Press, New York, 1997). The function of the educational institution is to transmit the cultural heritage from generation to generation, to teach the necessary skills in order to make the child an independent member of society.

The function of education, said Durkheim, is to integrate the individual into society. It is especially true about families of immigrants where children teach their parents the language of their new country. This view of the functionalist has been criticized by some sociologists who view education as a means to enforce the status quo while leaving the underclass, which needs it most, behind.

While education preserves the cultural heritage, it is also a vehicle of social change since it provides a marketplace for ideas. And ideas are like a pebbles in a pond: one never knows how far the ripples may go. Samuel Eisenstadt compared higher education to social movement, for its powerful ability to bring change.

As immigrants interact with their new culture, both immigrants and culture change in the process.

connie pertuz

"**t**ell me a story, Abuelo," I ask my 96-year-old grandfather, José Angel Pertuz. This is not an uncommon question I ask. When I was small and vacationing in Colombia in the summer, I would crawl on his lap and ask the same question. Now, when I ask my grandfather, I stretch my leg on his lap, though he insists I'll never be too big to sit on his old knees; I don't tell him but I agree secretly.

Why do you wear jeans Connie?, he questions with disapproval at the sight of my jeans-clad legs. How can you show those beautiful legs by having them wrapped up. Your abuela had some pair of legs, you know that's why I married her. I laugh to myself remembering that last week he said he married her for the great coffee she made and the week before that, for the way she looked in red. I know very well that he married her because he loved her and everything about her, but stay quiet. He continues to speak of her, how much he still misses her twenty years after her death, especially now that he's in this wretched place—the United States. I remind him that he's only going to be here for another four months and he had to come because of his surgery. He ignores my comment and complains further about this crazy country where the days drag endlessly. He theorizes that there must be something in this insane American air to keep the days longer so the people work more and make more money. I think to myself, it's believable—Americans will do anything for money.

So what story do you want me to tell you? he asks remembering my question. I ask him to tell me anything to get me to know him better. He looks up at me, his eyes squinted in thought, the same way my father stares when he's about to deliver a lecture on coming home late to me or my sister. I had never realized how many mannerisms my abuelo and father share and how I squint when I'm preparing to talk at length as well. It will take more than just a story to get to know me better—it'll take a life, he says. No, I am not a fascinating man, just an interestingly complicated one, he declares, staring straight ahead and not at me. He points to the bookcase in the room and tells me he has written many of those—books.

I stare at the books and at him, then ask him to read one of them to me. I don't question his sanity or his truthfulness, though I know this man knows neither how to read or write—I just ask him to tell me a story. This time when I ask there is no digression or pauses, only the words of the book page to page.

"I started writing in my head only when insomnia struck me as a boy, then I just wrote whenever I wasn't asleep—and even then I also wrote with my dreams." This is how one of his many books began, and it instantly became my favorite line. He didn't write because it was some poetic passion that took control of his senses and needed constant release. It was a defense against the boredom of his dull town, a drug to cloud the pain of hard work as a boy and the suffering as a man, a method to distract his hungry siblings from the emptiness of their bellies. It was his weapon of survival against the hardship that life gave him. This gift of storytelling wasn't always a blessing. He would pray to God that his imagination would burn out and there would be no more stories to tell. It was much too painful to live in stories as a king with great wealth and then in reality be without food for days—it was torture. God never did answer his prayers, thankfully, and he continued to write.

It was his ability to tell a story of animals that could speak, murdered people who came back from the dead to save another person from the hands of the murderer, love affairs that never quite worked out as expected and other stories that persuaded my abuela to be courted by my abuelo. "She had me tell her two stories every time I called on her," my abuelo recalls happily. My abuela insisted that one story be told early during my abuelo's visit, the other at the end. The first story selection could be varied according to her fancy—love story, fantasy, drama, comedy; the second story must be mystery. My abuelo never solved the mystery for my abuela until the next visit, so my abuela could try solving it on her own. She never was able to solve a mystery, but my abuelo muses she solved them every time. The reason she never told him the conclusion of the story was that she liked him to tell it. If it wasn't for the gift of storytelling, my abuelo believes he would have kept admiring my abuela from a distance—she wouldn't have given him a second glance. The day she died she had my abuelo tell her a story, a funny one, so she could tell God and make him laugh.

My father would never have gotten the stitches he needed for a serious cut on his leg when he was 8 if my abuelo hadn't kept him distracted with a story about angels who travel around the world trying to change mean-spirited hearts to kind ones, the same story my father told me when I had my tonsils taken out. The story was comforting and engrossing, not so much the plot but the beautiful details that illustrate the story in my mind. The expression in my father's eyes when he told me that story when I was 10 was identical to my abuelo's bright and passionate eyes when he's telling a story. Their voices also are similar, soothing and soft, painting another world with their sound.

In essence what makes my abuelo a great storyteller is not these stories of his own invention but how he works with these stories. It is how he makes you feel. When my abuelo tells me my favorite story of the mystical beauty of his childhood town, "Rosa The Marvelous," I can smell her jasmine-scented hair, feel her honey-soft skin, hear her harp-sounding voice—I become this magical Rosa. This is the gift that brings a crowd of people to my abuelo's home in Colombia at night to hear these stories. These people come to my abuelo's porch to become "Rosa The Marvelous" or Umberto, her heroic and charming lover. It's an escape to my abuelo's world of imagination, where it feels safe and comforting.

Unfortunately I was only able to touch on a few moments of my abuelo's book. It would be not a paper but a novel if I had written about all of abuelo's book, an autobiography that allowed me to see my abuelo in a different scope—as a writer who has come to accept his talent. So, through the joy it brings others, the "what if?" question "what if?" is lurking around, what if my abuelo had been able to write his books? Simple, my abuelo would be Colombia's finest writer along with Gabriel Garcia Marquez.

lissette wilkes

this paper is about an interview I did on two people who are very important to me: my grandparents. I could not interview them in person, because they are both dead, but I was told part of their life story by my mother. For this reason, I will not be able to go into much detail of their lives.

My grandparents lived in Trinidad and Tobago. At the time Trinidad and Tobago was like most third world countries: poor. This meant that most people did not receive a great deal of education because they were forced to leave school at an early age to take care of their families any way they could. Since there were not a lot of high-paying jobs for people who did not have a high degree of education, people had to try to make money and do whatever they could to survive. This is what my grandparents had to do. To survive and provide for their nine daughters, they had to go to extreme measures. For example, they had to sell bottles to earn money. Sometimes they even had to go to the city dump to find things that were useful. This interview is mainly based on how they provided for their children's education and other needs.

Even though my grandparents did not receive a lot of formal education, it does not mean that they were not smart. The exact amount of education my grandfather had is not

known by my mother, but she does know he went to secondary school. After he finished secondary school, he attended a
trade school and received training as a steel bender. He had
a job as a steel bender for one of the local steel companies
until he was laid off. As for my grandmother, being the
oldest one in her family, she had to leave school at an early
age to take care of her brother and sisters. She had to do this
because her mother had died. Whatever education she had
received she put to good use. She taught her brother and
sisters to read and write. She had to do the same for her own
children because at the time they could not afford to send
their children to school. My mother remembers how my
grandmother used to take her and her other sisters on the
porch and teach them. She would teach them to read with
the used books she had gotten from people in the neighborhood. To teach them to write, my grandmother would use a
piece of chalk and a small blackboard to show them how to
form their words. She would also hand out pencils and
pieces of paper for them to practice on.

My grandparents also did everything they could to
provide for their children's physical needs. After being laid
off from the local steel company, the only job my grandfather
had was selling bottles. Every morning at six my grandfather would go in search of discarded bottles. Sometimes he
would take two of his daughters with him to help out. He
would walk for miles looking for bottles. Then he would
wash and clean them before taking them to the rum factory
in the city. Here he would have to wait for hours while the
bottles were weighed and priced. Whatever money he received from the sale would go toward payment for any
goods or supplies that were needed. When he got home in
the afternoon he would have to take care of the few animals
that the family owned, which included pigs, chickens, a cow
and a donkey. He would have to feed the animals and clean

out their pens. After all the animals were taken care of, he would wash up, eat dinner and then go straight to bed. This was his routine every day except Sunday. On Sunday he would stay home and rest while the rest of the family went to church.

My grandmother also did her part when it came to contributing to the needs of the family. During the day when my grandfather was out selling bottles, she would take two of her daughters with her to the "labiss," or city dump. Here, with their help, she looked for whatever useful items were thrown out by people much richer than they. They would spend hours in the hot sun looking through the garbage to see what they could find. Whatever was found would be washed and then put to use in the house. Sometimes when pieces of cloth were found she would take them home, wash them, and then make garments for her children to wear.

In doing this interview I learned things that I had not known about my grandparents from my mother. Although I knew that we were poor, I did not know to what extent. I did not know that they had to turn to the city dump and selling discarded bottles in order to provide for their children. I did not know all these things even though I had lived with them for the first twelve years of my life. What I do know and remember about my grandparents is that they were a very hard-working couple and even though we did not have a lot of money, we did have a lot of love. I'm not ashamed of what my grandparents did in order to provide for their children; in fact, I'm very proud. I'm proud because their doing what they did shows me that their love was greater than their pride.

ann foley

For this assignment I interviewed my mother since both sets of my grandparents are dead. We spoke of her birthplace, the games she played with her siblings, her harrowing school years, her father's illness, work briefly, and finally about dating my father. The merriment and sense of fun she always exhibited when we were young were evident throughout her story.

My mother was born in 1929 in a small rural village in the south of Ireland. She and her family lived in a modest house with a thatched roof that her father built. She didn't have many toys, but she could recall a go-cart, which her father built for her, and a doll. Card games were a major part of their play growing up as the Irish weather is often very harsh and not at all accommodating to youngsters who long for the outdoors. When the weather did cooperate, however, my mother along with her sister and two brothers liked nothing better than wandering the fields and playing down by the River Blackwater. In the summertime one of their favorite things to do was to help the farmers bring in the hay from their fields. They were rewarded for their help with a spin in the farmer's horse and cart. My mother's voice grew lively and happy as she spoke of those times in the horse and cart; it was easy to conjure up an image of her as an energetic young girl working in the fields happy and carefree.

At the age of 6 my mother went off to the village school. This school was actually just one big room with a fireplace up at the front (they were still always frozen). All the grades, from babies (kindergarten) through the leaving cert (last year of high school), conducted their lessons in this one schoolhouse. My mother's early years at school were happy enough. All this changed, however, when my mother advanced to fourth class. The next several years were torture. She and her seven classmates were subjected to daily beatings and were in a constant state of terror, never knowing when their teacher would pounce. My mother could not recall one time when she saw this woman smile. There was a big map of the world on one wall of the room and students were frequently asked to point out particular places. If an unfortunate student gave the wrong answer, she could expect to have her head bashed against the wall have her hair pulled as the teacher flew into a fit of rage. One story in particular showed the comradeship of the students against this tyrant. My mother did something wrong one day (she could not remember what exactly) and as you can imagine she was paralyzed in fear of being found out. The teacher demanded that the students reveal the culprit. But no one would tell on my mother, knowing only too well what she would face if they did. As a result they all got a wallop from a bamboo stick that the teacher kept at hand. "Imagine that," my mother said, "and those were hard wallops too."

I asked her to tell me all she could about World War II. It surprised me to hear that she and her siblings felt very removed from the war. But she reminded me that they were, after all only children. She could recall a shortage of food and things like tea, sugar, and butter being rationed, but this did not bother them much.

A sad blow hit her family when she was 10 years old. Her father, a carpenter, developed Parkinson's disease and could no longer support his family. This was a very hard blow to the spirit of a proud man. He became very bitter and angry. However, my mother recalls fondly the father of her younger days: a man she was absolutely mad about. After this devastating blow her mother took over and managed to make ends meet. They had a few cows and some pigs and chickens. They sold milk to the creamery, fattened the pigs and sold them at the market where they then bought piglets for the following year. They reared the chickens, sold the cocks to the butcher and kept the hens for their eggs.

When she got older my mother loved to go dancing. She and her friends would cycle into the village on a Sunday night to go to a dance. Sometimes if a good band was in the area, they might go dancing three nights on the trot, hitching rides from friends if it was too far to cycle. She had great fun at those dances.

It struck me as strange then to hear that my father hated dancing and simply refused to go. They went instead to see Gaelic sports such as Gaelic football and hurling and the odd time they headed to the greyhound racing track. A friend had introduced them while my mother was living away from home (quite near my own hometown) and work-ing as a housekeeper. Their courtship lasted seven years and was only interrupted when my mother returned home to stay with her mother while she was ill. There was no roman-tic proposal or anything of that sort. It was just understood, she said, that they would marry.

When I first approached my mother concerning this interview she thought it an odd exercise and could not see its value. I knew that she had always dismissed such inquir-ies in the past as irrelevant. However, as I hounded her with questions, she gladly racked her brain to come up with memories. Because my mother lives in Ireland, I conducted this interview by phone. I noticed that with each phone call she became more and more interested in sharing her memories and even lay awake at night going through her childhood. In an excited voice she told me about arranging her dad's books, something she had not thought of in years. While my assignment is now complete, I know my mother and I will continue to chat about her life before she became my mother. Something has been awakened.

seɔgwick iyasere

my grandfather died when my father was 21 years old. This made it impossible for me to interview my grandfather. My grandmother is still alive, but she lives in Nigeria. So I decided to interview my father to tell me about his parents and about himself and my mother.

My father came to the United States in June 1974 to continue his educational studies. He said there were too few Nigerian universities at that time to admit the numerous applicants. He had to apply for a student visa for study in America. He achieved admission to. New York University.

My father first met my mother when she came from Benin city to Urhonibe (the village of both my father and my mother) on her holiday in 1965. At that time my mother was in high school and my father was in teachers' training college. They dated between 1965 and 1971 and then got married.

My father grew up in the late '40s and '50s. As a kid his life was very interesting and enjoyable because he was able to play with his many brothers and sisters. My father used to work with his dad and two brothers on the family farm where they grew food to eat and sell. He was the second son among his parents' children and there was another male just after him.

My late grandfather worked in a Nigerian hardwood company. He also had a farm where his children worked as soon as they came from their jobs at the hardwood company. My grandfather was very interested in getting his children to school. There was no school in the village where my father and my grandfather were living, so my grandfather sent his first son, Andrew, to school in Agbor and sent my father to school in Obiamku. My father's younger brother was asked to remain home for two years before he started school because there was no money to send all three brothers to school at the same time. In those days most parents did not want to send their children to school because it was very expensive, but my grandfather was able to send three of his children to school. My father and grandfather were both very hard working. During his holiday, my father had to work to be able to pay his school fees.

My father talked about the differences between life in Nigeria and the United States. In Nigeria you cannot combine studies with work as you can here. With few universities in Nigeria people there are forced to study a major that they are not interested in. The United States enjoys far greater opportunities.

My father decided he wanted four children because my late grandfather was married to four wives. My father's mother was the first wife of my grandfather and she had seven children, four males and three females. The second wife had two children, the third wife had six and the fourth wife had one child. All together my grandfather had sixteen children. Before he died, my grandfather expressed regret over having many wives and children because it was difficult to support them. He had to depend on his eldest sons—my father and his older brother—to help him feed the family. When my father saw the difficulties involved in having many children, my father and my mother decided to have only four kids.

My father left the United States for Nigeria immediately after graduating because my sister and I were in Nigeria. His reason for leaving in the first place was to go to school in the United States and once that was done, it was time to go home and get a better job. As a matter of fact, when my father got home he was offered a job in a bank as an auditor, a position that would have been very difficult for him to obtain in the United States. He survived in the United States by working while he was a student. My mom was also working and going to school at that time. My father said he and my mother were a happy couple. They trusted each other. It was that love and trust that tied them together.

My father grew up in a polygamous home. He said he and the rest of the children farmed together, worked together and came home to eat together. Only my grandfather's wives ate separately. My daddy and his brothers and sisters usually ate with my grandfather. My father said that eating together at that time showed togetherness among the family, even though sometimes there were differences either between the children or between my grandfather's wives. No matter what the problem was, my grandfather always gave the final decision, which everybody obeyed.

My father said he grew up in a village that lacked the basic amenities such as good water, electricity, telephone, etc. He also said that life in the village was devoid of fear. There were no drugs, no fear of being shot or robbed. My father said that they had sufficient food to eat and they were very happy.

It has been a great experience for me to interview my father because I now know things that I did not know about my grandparents and about my parents.

albert kim

he Korean War was the greatest event in the lives of my parents and all Koreans who were alive during that time period. Encyclopedias and textbooks tell us about a war between democracy and communism. After World War II, Korea was occupied by Soviets in the north and Americans in the south. In 1947, the UN decided that elections would be held to create one government, but the north was prohibited by the Soviets from holding elections. The south went ahead and elected a government in 1948, thus creating the Republic of Korea. Later that year, communists in the north created the Democratic People's Republic of Korea. Soon, both sides wanted control over the entire country. In 1949, the U.S. pulled its troops out of South Korea. Minor clashes occurred between the north and south until June 25, 1950, when South Korea was invaded by communist North Korean troops.

My father was about 10 when the fighting began. He was living in Seoul and was forced to leave his home and possessions. He and his family, consisting of his father, mother, sister and three brothers, walked for five days to the country, where they would be safe from the fighting. His father and sister immediately went back to the house in Seoul. There they found that anything of value had been stolen. Three months later, the U.S. army had taken Seoul and it was safe for the family to reunite.

On January 4, 1951, the Chinese army invaded Seoul, and the family was forced to flee to Taegu province in the southern part of South Korea. They traveled two hundred miles by train. My father recollected the image of the train loaded down with people and their possessions. People had to ride on top of the trains and if the train came to an abrupt halt, people fell off and sometimes died. There were very few railroad tracks, and so the army got preference in their use. Long periods of time went by before the people could get moving again so the progress of the civilians was slowed.

On arrival in Taegu, things got worse. The family was forced to sleep in an open market where there was at least a roof to cover their heads. The market was occupied by an enormous number of people, all fleeing the war. Later, the family purchased a small hut in a corner of a vegetable farm. The small hut was constructed of burlap, and my father could remember many sleepless nights. He felt it was strange seeing the stars and moon through the walls of his house. Money was scarce, so my father did anything he could to make money. He worked in a dishmaking factory, and in his spare time he bought metal and made dishes at home. He also bought several items such as cigarettes and gum, and carried them around in a large box, selling them to the GI's and other people, while his mother and sister sold items in the open market. Through much hardship, they were able to survive, but the hard life took its toll on my father's mother. A year after their arrival, she died.

In 1953, an armistice was signed, and the fighting was over. The family came back to Seoul for the second time, but life was not as it had been. Prior to the war, my grandfather had been a dish salesman, but all of his merchandise had been destroyed or stolen during the war. Times were hard, and my father had nothing to wear but long underwear. My grandfather was able to become the custodian for Korea University, which provided a house for him and his family. My father had been unable to complete his last year of elementary school because of the war. He discouraged and refused his father's suggestion that he return to school. Instead be became an office boy for Korea University. He continued to work there, and soon began to go to school at night. He completed three years of school in two years, and was able to catch up to his own class. He also went to high school at night after working in the day.

In 1959, my father entered Korea University. Before his junior year began, he had a decision to make. All Korean males are required to serve in the military, and my father could either serve for three years after graduating college or serve one and a half years after completing his sophomore year. He opted for the shorter time in the army. He received basic training and spent many nights living in improvised barracks with straw roofs, in the mountains. He also spent some time in the DMZ (demilitarized zone) clearing roads and digging trenches. Unfortunately, in 1962 my grandfather lost his job with Korea University just as my father had completed his stint in the military. For the next two years, my father and his family were forced to move around from place to place, until my father received his B.S. in physics.

My father spent the next couple of years teaching physics in a high school in the countryside. He was now the main source of income for his family. On August 22, 1967, my father returned to Seoul to say goodbye to a friend who was leaving to study in America, but that same day, my father's father died. The untimely deaths of his parents were my father's saddest moments.

My father began teaching at a school in Seoul, and in 1971 met the new school nurse, who was to become my mother. In 1972, she left for the U.S., but they kept in contact

by writing letters to each other. In 1974, she returned to
Korea and they were married. Soon after, they both returned
to the U.S., taking the one-day flight that stopped over in
Tokyo, Hawaii, and Los Angeles. Finally they ended up in
Brooklyn, New York.

My mother was born in Seoul and was about 4 when the
fighting started. She didn't remember much, but what she
did remember was similar to my father's story, and probably
similar to the stories of all Koreans caught up in the Korean
War. My mother and her family left their house in Seoul and
fled to the south. They rented a car and ended up somewhere near Chonan province. They rented a small room and
had to cram ten people into it. They found out that their
house and possessions had been blown up by a bomb. My
mother and her family remained in the south for three years,
and then moved back to Seoul. My mother's main memories
of that time period were of playing in the river while my
grandmother washed clothes and also of asking the GIs for
gum and candy. It is interesting that despite having to live
through the war and experiencing all its horrible consequences, my mother's saddest moment came in August 1992
when her sister died of cancer.

In 1965, my mother entered Seoul National University,
the most prestigious college in Korea. She graduated with a
B.S. in nursing. After graduating, she worked in the college's
attached hospital in the medical unit. In 1971, she went to
work in O'san High School where she became the school
nurse and also where she met my father. In May of 1972, my
mother came to the U.S. on a permit and began working at
the Suffolk State School for the Mentally Retarded. A year
later, my mother took and passed the state board test, and
officially became an R.N. She then went back to Korea to
marry my father. They returned to New York, and she has
since been working at Coney Island Hospital.

The Korean War threw the lives of all Koreans into disarray. The war sent the lives of my parents in the same direction. Both of them had to flee and both ended up working in the same high school. It is only natural that they both came to the U.S. looking for better lives and eventually to provide their children with all the opportunities they never had. On a different note, a permanent peace treaty has never been agreed upon between North and South Korea, but talks were recently held in New York City.

CARLA MARIE GOMILLA

During his homily at a 12:30 Mass on a previous Sunday, Father Francis said, "There is only one place where success comes before work...in the dictionary." That too applies to my paternal grandmother's life. With the advice she gave me during our interview, I acknowledge that she too would agree with Father Francis. She said, "My advice to you, as a growing person: whatever you do, finish whatever you are doing until you realize your goal in life." In doing that, my grandmother assured me success.

On May 21, 1923, Isabelita Vargas Geaga, or Lola [loh-la] (grandma in the Filipino language) Diting [dee-ting], was born at her parents' house in Ilog [ee-loog] (a small town in the southern region of Negros Occidental). She says she was brought up in "a very strict, Catholic, disciplinarian home." "[Her] father, Segundo, a postmaster, enforced discipline for all the children" and [her] mother, Mercedes, a property holder, remained "very reserved" in order to "help in the molding of the [children's] characters."

Lola Diting, along with her four sisters and two brothers, had their fair share of household chores, but were encouraged to focus more on their religious and academic lives. Recalling her childhood, Lola began, "Sunday Mass obligations were without fail. The family said the Holy Rosary every night." Never did Lola or her brothers and sisters neglect their homework, not because of the grave consequences but because it was expected of them. Teachers "would double the assignments or make students kneel on dried mongo[1] beans" if he or she failed to do his or her work due that day. This would happen on rare occasions, because "back in the Philippines, the atmosphere was more disciplined, orderly. The students never questioned the authority of the teacher, [they] were in acceptance of the teacher's instructions."

Lola having been raised in a stern, academic-oriented household, it is obvious that social activities were discouraged by her parents. She and her siblings were allowed to go to social functions, like parties, dances or shows, but only in groups. And if "[Lola or her sisters] were to go out when [they] were younger, [they] were always in accompaniment of [their] mother" and, later on, with either of their brothers. Playing sports was considered by Filipino parents at the time as activities only for boys. Lola's parents dissuaded her and her sisters. When referring to being a teenaged girl, Lola said, "It was against moral standards to have relations with boys."

Socializing was always the least of my studious grandmother's worries, even more so in that there was a war going on: World War II. It was a hazardous time in the tropical archipelago, especially because Clark Air Base, an American (the Allies[2]) base, was situated in the Philippines, then a commonwealth of the U.S. With the intention of conquering it, Japan, one of the Axis powers, invaded Lola's homeland. Although the actual fighting didn't occur where Lola lived but in neighboring cities, Lola's sisters and parents had to "evacuate [their] house ten times to run away from the Japanese," who came from the cities "to the barrios or villages." Lola added, "They were in search of young girls to rape." Her brothers were absent during their pursuit of a safe haven; one joined the Army, the other the guerillas. On their last evacuation, Lola Diting and her family "spent ten days walking along the mountainside from Ilog, a coastal town, to Sipalay (See-pah-lie), a town further south and even further in the mountains." "In the middle of the night, we prayed," Lola recalls. They managed to avoid the Japanese. However, they returned only to discover that their house had been burned down and their belongings taken.

During the war, it was customary for off-duty Army officers to visit the civilians at home. One of those officers would be my grandfather, Lolo Emilio. Lolo courted my grandma for several years, even to the end of the war. One day, my grandpa came back and asked Lola for her hand in marriage. "Being true to [her] promise, [she] soon became Mrs. Isabelita Gomilla." She married Lolo in her third year of college. Being a supportive husband, he agreed to pay for her education until she graduated—even though she would be attending school in Manila, a city on another island.

"Under excellent, interesting and very caring teachers" all throughout her education, Lola Diting's "dream and aspiration of becoming a teacher" finally became a reality. After graduating cum laude with a B.S. degree in education from the University of the Philippines, the highest academically regarded state university in the country, Lola followed my grandpa to where he was teaching. At Kawayan [ka-wa-yahn] (a branch of Kabankalan [kah-bahnk-ka- lan] Academy), Lolo Emilio taught general science, mathematics and biology, while Lola Diting taught English composition, English literature and history. Later, Lola was assigned as principal of the high school department. And soon after she finished her master's in education, she took the position of dean at Binalbagan Catholic College.

Lolo didn't mind that Lola was working. Aside from his being a firm believer in women in the workforce, there was a great need of double-income families, since the cost of living was steadily increasing in the Philippines. Not only that, but there were many additions to the family: Julian Segundo, Maria Araceli, Alberto Jesus, Raymond Francis, Maria Lourdes, Jaime Valentine, Luis and Maria Magdalena.

"After all the children finished their studies and the death of [my] Lolo in 1980, the economic condition in the Philippines was not conducive to job placement." Lola's two eldest daughters, who were both nurses and living in New York, "convinced the whole family to join them in the land of opportunities. So, we came." After all my aunts, uncles and dad came to America, the three of us together—Lola, my mom and I—soon followed.

"Money cannot buy everything," Lola Diting declares, "...so values we have imbibed back home, like strong family solidarity, a sound religious foundation, family cooperation among the members, respect and consideration for individual differences, and a lot of moral values, we are sorry to admit, are absent in this seemingly land of paradise." She continues, "There are so many things here like dignity of work, opportunities of success, equality before the law, abundance of food, clothing, comfort and convenience in one's lifestyle everything—if you have the money to buy.... In terms of material, scientific progress—medical and health care services—America is tops."

"I think I accomplished my mission to my eight children, who turned out to be successful in their respective careers." In that way, Lola has accomplished what she sought, but then she adds, "I have almost realized my dreams in life and my only dream is to die a happy, holy and peaceful death. Amen."

Lola, in many ways, has taught me very important lessons. But the most important one she has taught me need not be said aloud: To live a meaningful, prosperous and well-lived life. After all:

> It's good to have
> an end to a journey
> towards; but in the end,
> it is the journey itself
> that makes the
> difference.
>
> - Ursula K. Le Guin[3]

---

[1] mongo— a Filipino word for mung beans, a variety of small yellow or green beans.

[2] the Allies— the forty-nine countries allied against the Axis powers in the Second World War.

[3] *For My Daughter: Thoughts of Love, Life and Happiness,* Andrews and McMeel, Kansas City, 1993, p.21.

section iii
religious life

max Weber, in his classic study of *The Protestant Ethic and the Spirit of Capitalism*, showed us the fundamental relationships between religion and the economic and social life. Religion is a worldview which shapes the many aspects of the daily life of the believers. Countless historical circumstances cannot be reduced to any economic law, and are not given to economic explanation of any sort. The vision one has of the world defines man's position and his purpose on earth. Religion is a way of life, a guiding force, a set of moral values which for some are more important than life itself. Religious community binds society together and links one generation to another. It helps man feel at home in the world. Even in our secular world we may discover, deep down in our social memory, some religious roots. They die hard.

We tend to think of religion with reverence and awe. Durkheim saw religion as a binding force. Man expresses his beliefs by practicing the rituals, celebrating important events in personal and social life, like holidays and birth and marriage and death. Through religion we celebrate the individual's life and make it socially significant. The religious community recognizes the individual, stands behind him, protects him and helps him in periods of transition and in crises which are part of the human condition. All religions have rituals with symbolic representations of the sacred, the symbolic meaning of life.

Yet we tend to forget that religion not only binds us together, it breaks us apart. Much blood has been spilled in the name of God. "Religion is the sigh of the oppressed creature, the sentiment of the heartless world, and the soul of the soulless condition. It is the opium of the people," wrote Karl Marx*. Some grandparents still remember religious persecutions and how they persisted to practice their religion secretly. *(*Selected Writings*, translated by T.B. Bottomore, New York: McGraw-Hill, 1964 p. 26)

On an individual level Erik Erikson advises us that "the clinician can only observe that many are proud to be without religion whose children cannot afford their being without it" (*Childhood and Society*, W. W. Norton, New York, 1963, p. 251).

Robert Bellah (*Beyond Belief*, Harper and Row, New York, 1970) describes modern religious life as the Civil Religion, yet many religious communities persist and their members still maintain their religious identities and shared memories, maintain some religious practices and neglect others, even when they have a problem defining their identities.

Included in this collection are papers which tell stories some may not consider religious in a Western sense. They discuss symbolic rituals regarding the dead or other family and community affairs. These rituals reflect the grandparents' world. We may find some rituals strange, a testimony of ethnocentrism which brings to mind the story of an American who saw a Chinese man in the cemetery placing a bowl of rice on the grave of his father. "When will your dead get up to eat the rice?" inquired the American. "The same time your dead will get up to smell the flowers," answered the Chinese man.

In the students' papers, they tell us that the church was the community center of social life, where worshipers came to meet their friends and celebrate personal events of birth, death and marriage, where they showed off their new hats and where they heard all the fresh gossip, met their dates and sang in the chorus. The best times of their lives were the church holidays. Dressed in their Sunday best, they remember how they enjoyed the dress, food, color, smell and music. What is life without a holiday?

MARJORIE CORIOLAN

my name is Francoise Francois. I was born on January 9, 1913. I am an active 82-year-old woman who has lived with my daughter and son-in-law for years, helping them raise their seven kids. I also take care of the household chores, making it possible for them both to work.

Despite my health problems in the past, the Lord has blessed me with renewed health and vigor. I was hospitalized at Brookdale Hospital for diabetes, not long after I came to New York from Haiti. I had not known I was diabetic until it was almost too late. Two other times I was operated on for kidney problems which left me with one kidney. However, those problems did little to slow me down. I am not a lazy person; neither am I the type of person who likes to give in to illnesses; I like to overcome them.

My toughness has a lot to do with the way I was raised as a child. I had to labor hard in my lifetime to survive. I grew up in Tomazo, an area in the countryside of Haiti. My family and the people of that area worked hard farming to make a living. I was one of six children, which my mother had with my father. We lived with my mother, since our father was married to someone else. He visited us once in a while, taking care of us the best way he could.

On a typical day, the cock crowed at four in the morning, announcing the beginning of a new day. I would wake up to the sound and go bathing in the river. Upon my return, I cleaned the house, fixed up the table, fixed up my bed and drank coffee.

If I had provisions to sell at the market, I would go sell them. Otherwise I stayed home to work, cook and lie down to rest.

In the neighborhood, everyone remained in their own homes when they were not out working on their crops. We would open up a blanket on the floor, with fresh rice spread out on it. We would watch the rice, making sure that pigs and chickens did come eat it.

When I needed fresh meat, I would send a few people out to kill animals for me. I would clean them with sour lemons, salt them up, put them out in the sun to dry. Some of the meat I had was cow meat. After it was dried, I would gather it up, then fill a high barrel with the meat. Part of the meat would be sold out, piece by piece.

Some mornings, I untied my donkey from its post; so I could go work on the crops. I would plant a variety of seeds in the rich soil, like herbs, okra, rice, peas, potatoes and maize. At harvest time, I would gather whatever the crops yielded, cutting them up from their roots. A lot of people would assist me at the time. In return for their labor, I gave them a fair amount of provisions. These were some of the things I was able to do best besides cooking and caring for myself and my family.

Unfortunately, one thing I lacked was education. When I was young, my mother tried to make me go to school. I didn't understand anything. I was scared and ran to hide. I never went to school, neither did my four siblings.

Now I realize school would have been good for me. I have become old and don't have that opportunity anymore. I can count money because of my former experience in selling and buying. But I am unable to read and write. Many times I tried to write my name and my granddaughter tried to teach me. Each time she taught me how to write a letter of my name I would forget again. The letters refused to stay in my memory.

I have learned too late in life the importance of education. It is a useful tool for anyone to have an opportunity to go to school and make something of themselves; they should not throw it away. I always encouraged my grandchildren to go to school and to listen to their parents. I would say, "Kids, know that you are kids. When your parents tell you something, listen—because you are just coming. You don't know nothing about life yet."

When I was a child, my mother didn't want me to go out. She didn't want me to go dancing , drinking, smoking and partying. She also did not want me to have any friends because of the trouble that often came along. I listened to her and remained at home. I never liked to play. The thing I enjoyed doing the most was to dress up on special occasions. I would wear heels and comb my hair up.

On one of these occasions, I went up and met Denis Vieus at his office. I had accompanied a friend who needed him to plead a case for her. He was a very influential man because of the positions he held in Tomazo. He was a magistrate of Tomazo, a notarizer and a lawyer. He traveled often.

The first time he set eyes on me, he liked me. He repeatedly said, "Good morning, Miss." I said, "I don't want nobody to come bothering me. The next thing I know you will leave me pregnant." To convince me of his noble intentions, he said repeatedly, "I'm an adult, it is my desire and will to be with you."

But, men are deceivers! I got involved with him and told my mother this man said he would do something for me. But he never married me. He was already married. He also had three other women as mistresses.

Denis continued living with his wife, visiting me on occasions. He had a visiting day for each of his mistresses. He gave me anything I wanted and a home. I trusted him and thought that he was going to leave his other women to marry me. I was very young at the time and he was much older than me. I stayed with him, not just because of the things he gave me. He treated me well. I liked the way he spoke and carried himself. I thought it was better to get involved with an educated man, who could take care of me, than to be involved with a vagabond. I never got involved with anyone else.

Whenever I came to Tomazo, I did my best to please him. I would boil giant pots of milk cleaning them out real well, so the milk would not spoil. When they were done, Denis had a number of things to store milk. I would also give him coals and all sorts of food from the crops. They would be poured in sacks, which I would sew with a giant needle. He would carry them to the other women and all our children in Port-au-Prince.

My children did not live with me. They lived in Port-au-Prince with Denis's relatives so they could go to school. They visited me at home when they were on vacation. We had nine kids together. Only three of our children survived. We lost the other six. Three of them became sick and died while they were babes in my hands. At one time, when I was pregnant, I bled and miscarried a set of twins. The last one died after I gave birth to him, through the malice of a mid-wife who usually helped me in labor.

She had bought rice from me and her money wasn't enough for the amount that she wanted. She said that I measured the rice wrong for her. I said, "If I measured the rice for you and your money is not enough, it's not me. I will give you another rice." She was angry and silently sought revenge. I was pregnant at the time and she planned on using that time for revenge.

When the time came for me to have the baby, she purposely cut the child's navel cord wrong. She left me with the baby crying relentlessly, and rant straight to the cemetery. I sent for her to help me with the child, who kept crying; she refused to come. My godson saw her at the cemetery while he was passing by. He heard her speaking to the loas that she served. She told the loas what I did to her and she wanted revenge. She told Baal, the loa she served, what she did to my child. She said she wanted it to take the child's soul. My godson came to tell me what happened. No wonder she ignored me and the child. The child did not stop crying until he finally died.

A person can't trust anyone. She made me lose my child. Oh, God! People do suffer. This was a very painful moment for me as were my other losses. I suspect that the other children I lost also died from unnatural circumstances, because I came from a family and lived in an area where people spent most of their lives practicing voodoo magic and serving the loas. Family members and friends will kill each other out of jealousy to gain what each other has. Even if they knew they couldn't have it, they take yours away until you remain empty-handed. A stranger who is unfamiliar with some of the religious practices of Haitians, who has not lived those experiences, would not understand. I hate the way my family and I had to suffer from them.

Denis didn't understand the things I went through. He never knew how these six children died so rapidly. All he knew was that they were gone. He had a lot more children with his other women. Except for his wife, who never had any children with him.

Denis died before his wife who died of cancer. Like myself, Denis was diabetic. He used to travel to New York every year, in July, to see a doctor. He prescribed him a lot of medicine. But it wasn't his diabetes that actually killed him. He would not have died so soon.

Denis' parents had raised him strictly, so he raised all his children strictly. He was severe in his punishment. As a result, his children respected him. He did not want to pay for school for all his children. But he paid for school for my children. They had to earn their rights to finish school by getting high school diplomas. If they failed their courses, they would be punished.

He had a daughter named Annette with a woman of his called Elaine. Annette became pregnant with a child. He became upset when he found out and lost his temper. To him, no daughter of his should be pregnant without being married. He kept arguing and claimed that he was going to throw Annette out of the house. When Elaine realized that he seriously planned on throwing Annette out, she planned voodoo magic on him.

Denis had gone to Tomazo to see me. On his way back, something took over his car, almost turning it over. He left and went to Port-au-Prince. His sugar level rose immensely. The same moment the voodoo spell touched him, he became dumb, unable to speak. He had to make signs with his hands when he needed to say something. One day, while he was in his office, he became worse. He was trembling very badly. Our young son, Velten, and someone else took him to the hospital. The doctors couldn't do anything to improve his condition. He spent a long time in the hospital until he died.

My son picked me up from Tomazo, to bring me to Port-au-Prince. When I got there I stayed with my only daughter, Jeannise, and her husband. She had three children at the time. While I was there, I got the news that Denis had died. I was surprised at the news and cried. Denis' wife took care of the funeral. I have lived with my daughter ever since, going to Tomazo once in a while.

Rashell Clarke

uriel MacDonald was born in Epsom, Jamaica, in the West Indies. The year was 1929. Epsom is a small rural community, one mile from the main road and five miles from the nearest town. Muriel, my grandmother, is the youngest child of Albertine and Augustus Marshall. Her mother was a housewife and her father was a farmer. He was also a deacon in the local church. Muriel was born at home, like most children at the time, by a midwife (her "Nana"-grandmother). She grew up with an older sister (her mother's child) and a cousin. Three of her siblings died at a very young age. Being the only surviving child of her father, she was pampered

Her parents insisted on her going to school until the ninth grade (third book, as it was called then). She was about 15 or 16 when she finished school. I asked her what her first day of school was like. She told me that the only thing she could remember about it was that her teacher gave her a nickname. Her teacher called her "One Ton" because she was fat. The name stuck with her all through her childhood. There was no celebration of her finishing school—it was not a part of the custom.

She also spoke of two dolls she had as a little girl. One was made from rooted grass which was plaited. The root was used as the head of the doll. The other doll was made of cloth which was stuffed with a cottonlike material. A face was painted on the cloth and strands from a crocus bag were sewed to the cloth. These strands were the doll's hair. She was very proud of her dolls, which she made herself.

However, she was unable to play with the dolls until her chores were completed. Her chores included running errands for her mother, helping around the house and helping her father on the farm.

In her spare time she would also play the organ which her father had bought for her. She insists that the entire community was jealous of her because she was the only one in the community who owned an organ. Not even the two churches in the community had an organ. When her school years were over, she would walk five miles to the nearest town for music and sewing lessons.

My grandmother does not remember any birthday celebrations as a child. Birthdays were not emphasized because parents did not want their children (especially girls) to know how old they were. Parents believed that a child who knew that she was getting to be an adult would want to behave like one.

However, my grandmother remembers funerals very well. She remembers when one of her sisters died. She was about 6 years old. Her sister was buried two days after her death because it was believed that if the body was not buried before the third day, it would rise from the dead. She remembers the entire community coming to her house to sing each night for nine nights, after the child's death. This was called "setup." On the ninth night, there was a lot of food to eat and games to play. She remembers eating fried fish and bread with chocolate tea. When her sister was being buried, white rum was poured around the hole to ward off evil spirits. The interior of the house was rearranged in case the dead came back. By the rearranging of the house, the dead would not recognize it and, therefore, not enter the house. Something, she does not remember what it was, was placed in the grave to keep the body "planted" there. She remembers this last act alleviating her fears that her sister might come back to haunt her.

My grandmother got married in 1949. Before she got married, John (her future husband) would come to her house pretending to be accompanying his sister, who was Muriel's friend. This happened for about a year. John eventually asked her parents for their daughter's hand in marriage and they said yes. My grandmother did not love him, but she consented after much pressure from her mother. She also thought she had no one better to choose from and John's parents were friends of the family and respected in the community. After their marriage, my grandmother became a housewife and John worked on his parents' farm. There was no honeymoon. When I asked her about her wedding day, she said she didn't wish for it to be mentioned in my class report. All she said was that her wedding day was not one of the happiest days in her life. I know from other sources that her father never agreed to the marriage and made Muriel's wedding day unbearable for her. She and her husband lived with her parents for five years after their marriage. This was not unusual for newly-weds.

My grandmother had ten children, but four of them died very young. When her children were babies, she would wrap an inch measure and place it in a red pocket which she had sewn. A band was sewed to the pocket and placed around the baby's arms to ward off evil. A Bible was also placed over the head while the baby was sleeping. The Bible had to be opened to any psalm which was also used to ward off evil. This was done until the child could move around on its own. When any of her children were ill, she would give them garlic burned in coconut oil or rub camphor (in coconut oil) on the child. The latter was used to clear stuffiness.

My grandmother's father died when she was 25 and although she is not proud of it, she was somewhat glad when he died. She thought he was very strict and selfish. She refused to comment more on it. It is considered wrong to speak ill of the dead. Two years after her father's death, she and her husband migrated to England. While in England, she became a physical therapist at the age of 50.

When I asked her the one thing she most regretted doing in the course of her life, she replied "marrying John" without any hesitation. Unlike her parents, she did not marry because of love, and although she tried, she could not love her husband. She never considered divorce an option because it was unheard of when she was growing up. However, after much pressure from her own children, she divorced John about two years ago. She is now living alone in Jamaica, far away from her family, although she keeps in contact with them. Why she prefers to live like this is still unknown. She refuses to tell anyone her reason.

The interview was actually more personal than what is told to the reader. However, my grandmother likes her personal life to be kept within her family. I was forced to omit many details because they were too personal and I knew I would be violating my grandmother's privacy if I told them to strangers.

This interview made me understand where some of my most important values come from and why my grandmother is who she is. Although I have only seen my grandmother a handful of times, this interview showed me how much I am like her.

ihab girgis

Unfortunately, my grandmother on my mother's side, with whom I would have wished to conduct an interview, passed away a few months ago. However, since I still remember her, I decided to write a biography of her. In the search for more facts about her life, I relied on my mother, who knew her very well. So this biography is mostly based on an interview with my mother, plus my own knowledge. The information I got access to couldn't have been derived from a format of questions and answers. When my mother agreed to help me on this task, she seemed as if she were engaging in a sacred ritual of telling her mother's story. Therefore, I didn't dare to disturb her flow of thoughts by asking questions, especially when she got into it. I tried hard to translate what she had said into English without distorting any information. She introduced her mother by mentioning her name and place of birth.

My mother's name was "Antoinette." She was born August 15, 1924, in the city of Alexandria, Egypt. She was the second child of four born to a couple named Samuel and Mariam. For the first eighteen years, she was raised in a nuclear family consisting of her parents, a brother and two sisters. Even though the family wasn't rich, they owned the house that they had inherited from the past generation. She grew up in the period when Egypt was under British rule. She used to tell me some of the horrifying stories of how innocent people died in the war. At that time, the Germans used to attack the British colonies from the air. Consequently, there were a lot of airplane raids, and we were the victims. She witnessed one of her best friends die in the war when an airplane dropped a bomb on their block. People hurried to hide in the basement whenever they heard the whistle or signal that indicated a possible air raid. Unable to face peril, she used to faint. She sometimes spoke of the political and social conditions that existed during her youth. She liked to talk about the political changes that occurred then. She was amazed at how the revolutionists, lead by Nasser, managed to overthrow the monarchy and replace it with a republic. She always mentioned how the end of British rule, in 1952, was a turning point in our history.

When she was a child, her parents sent her to a French Catholic school in order to get an education and to learn the fundamentals of religion. Even though Egypt was under British occupation, French was much more popular than English. Therefore, they wanted her to continue learning French, the language of the elite and the aristocrats.

At that time, people's everyday life revolved around the church. They were very religious. Their daily concern was to focus on the needs of the religious community. In other words, religious institutions guided and directed their lives. Church was a foundation of life. All familial and marital problems were solved with the help of the church. If a person had a personal problem of any sort, it was common for him or her to get help from a priest. Most of the picnics, trips and family outings were sponsored by the church. So it is fair to say that she was raised in a very religious community. Her parents made sure that she went to church with them every Sunday. They also made sure to deliver her to Sunday school to attend religion classes. I remember her telling me that she was an active participant in a "patronage" program, literally translated "the soldiers of Marie." The members were assigned different tasks each time such as visiting orphanages, helping the poor and visiting hospitals to distribute gifts to patients. In order to participate in this program, one had to show a great deal of enthusiasm and make a vow to stick to its rules. Religion and church played a big role in shaping people's ideas about the world.

Girls had many tasks to learn and perform. For example, learning how to sew, cook and take care of children were three basic skills that girls had to be good at in order to prepare for married life. Her life was a typical childhood of that period, meaning that her life was divided among church, school and home.

She got married to my father at the age of 19. He came to propose to her and the very next week they became husband and wife. She didn't have any right to agree or refuse. All she had to do was to wear the bridal gown, attend the marriage ceremony in church and then go home with her man. It was nothing like these modern days when people have a chance to meet and learn about each other. It might be startling to hear that even though people got married in this traditional way, there weren't any divorce cases. Husbands and wives didn't know each other before marrying, but they got along very well. There wasn't such a thing as divorce or separation.

My mother was secretly in love with another person before she got married. However, she couldn't go against her parents' will, or she would have been considered "deviant." Even though marrying the person she didn't prefer did not affect her role as a devoted mother and wife, this incident had a lasting influence on her. She always felt that women were helpless and hopeless. It was deplorable that she didn't get to choose the man she would spend the rest of her life with. I remember her saying, "The most important thing in life is to marry and be close to the beloved."

Since we were five children, she needed a great deal of money. My father's money wasn't enough to meet our financial needs. Therefore, she used her sewing skills and worked as a tailor on a machine she owned. Her dexterity in designing clothes made her very popular among the rich families. She worked hard to get as much money as possible. She didn't keep any money for herself but used all of it to satisfy our endless demands. Despite all the aggravation she faced in life, she was a very loving wife and a devoted mother. She raised all of us the way she was raised. She was concerned to teach us the religious values that she had learned. She sacrificed much to put all of us into Catholic schools. And finally she struggled to put us through college. She also encouraged me and my two brothers to pursue our graduate degrees and even provided us with most of the tuition money. She truly was a great lady. I will never forget her sacrifices.

After this sentence, I realized that my mother's tone of voice had changed. She spoke with great difficulty. Abruptly, she stopped talking, and her face displayed signs of affliction. There was a long pause accompanied by sighs. I realized that she couldn't go on. However, to wrap up the interview, I gently asked my mother to describe my grandmother in a few, simple words. She replied, with tears in her eyes, that "she was a magnificent individual—I hope to accomplish half of what she did." After this sentence, I stopped the interview and showed her signs of gratitude and appreciation for the help. In the meanwhile, I sought a way to add what I knew about my grandmother.

My grandmother had a direct and indirect impact upon me. She directly influenced me because I spent most of my childhood with her. As a matter of fact, I lived with her for approximately two years when my mother was away in France to pursue her graduate degree. I was very affected by her pleasant, kind nature. I remember that I was very much impressed with the way she did things. For example, she used to arrange the house, cook and take care of me all at once. She was so simple. She always had a smile on her face, and never complained or got angry. She had plenty of friends and acquaintances who loved and respected her. I also remember that she used to cook special kinds of food, especially the ones I showed preference for. Nothing seemed to affect her good temper because she was contented with what she had. She was always saying, "God didn't give me wealth, but gave me fine children and grandchildren." I remember that she used to read me various verses from the Bible and explain them to me in very simple language. To ensure learning, she was always concerned about explicitly pointing out the moral or lesson at the end of each of her anecdotes.

My mother used my grandmother's method to discipline me. She taught me everything she knew from her. She put me into a Catholic school. She was also very concerned to deliver me to church and Sunday school to instill in me religious values. It's really amazing how values are transmitted from one generation to another as if it's something inherited in the genes. It is not too much to say that almost everything my grandmother had learned during her childhood I eventually learned as well.

I was greatly disappointed when I left my grandmother in Egypt to immigrate to the United States. I was so attached to her that I asked her to come with us. However, she couldn't because she had to take care of her other grandchildren.

Last year, my grandmother managed to visit us. I spent a great deal of time talking to her. She was fascinated with how my thoughts had changed in just a period of five years. On the other hand, for the first time, I realized and was amazed that her experience far exceeded my humble education. I knew that I had learned very little compared to her great wisdom. However, she was still willing to listen to all of what I had to say with an open mind. I was very upset when she went back home, and I was even more upset to learn that she had died of cancer a few months later. All my family members were in a depressed, mournful mood for a long time. I knew that I had lost a great person, but meanwhile I was aware that we still retain her teachings. She left us with an immortal legacy that will always remind us of her significance. I was happy that we managed to see her again right before she died. To put it in my mother's words, "it was a divine arrangement that made us see her before God took her soul away."

faina zagorina

I am closing my eyes, and the train continues the regular motion carrying its six cars soundlessly and smoothly. It always goes in the same direction—forward, toward its point of destination—the future. I wish I could say that I know all the passengers: six cars are the six generations of my family; but I realize they embrace too many lives, names, feelings, events of which I am not aware, which have gone forever unattainable for me, and nothing and nobody in the whole world can fill and fix this gap today.

I am watching the train and it slows down under my steady gaze. The last car remains small and blurry—so dim and poor is information about the great-grandparents. All I know is that the old man, a rabbi in the small Ukrainian town of Kozelets, raised, together with his wife, ten sons and one daughter (my mother's mother) and died during World War II. Alas, I can say nothing at all about my father's grandparents: no photos, papers, stories, memories are available. So I am coming up to the fifth car where my own and my spouse's grandparents should be. And here, of course, I see her, my husband's grandmother, whom I am going to write about in my essay.

Amazingly small, thin, with short-cut gray hair, she might look like a 9-year-old girl if one could only ignore

113

those wizened hands and face, wrinkled, appallingly pale, drooped; those eyes, light, blurry, almost colorless. She seemed tired, emaciated, worn-out, incapable of feeling or, at least, expressing any strong emotions. As long as I knew her, she never cried, sobbed, yelled, laughed, raised her voice. It was obvious that energy and life were leaving her gradually. Indeed, after I came into her house when I married her grandson, she lived only one more year and died at 86 years of age, having predicted, "It will be a boy in three days and a very nice one."

Thus, here are the reasons why I chose her for the "life story of a grandmother" essay. First, we used to talk together, often and informally, and many of these conversations were about her time and life. Second, her last words were an almost superstitiously correct prediction: I was three months in Moscow, far from my home at that time, so—how could she know?—not only did I get a son, not only was he born three days after she died, but he strikingly resembled her. I remember even now the strange feeling, blend of delight and jealousy, upon seeing the mysterious and perfect job of genes; when I was looking at a baby's face I saw her, only her in it.

Now I think that in the face of such an obvious physical linkage the moral, cultural, social linkage should be even more important to find and keep.

Grandmother was born and lived for a very long time in the small Byelorussian town of Vetka, not far from the big city Gomel (where my husband and I were born and lived before emigration to America in 1991). Vetka was one of the places that were determined for Jews to settle in. Her uncle, she said, had to move to Poland after he found out that he could not acquire the skills of a lady's dressmaker in a big center, for Jews were not allowed, at that time, to live where the necessary workshops were available. Her own father was a furrier and the only breadwinner of a family with five children. She remembered that he worked hard and they lived hard. Nevertheless, they did not suffer from hunger as my father's family had; there was, for example, always something to eat. She remembered that at 4 or 5 years old she was asked to feed the geese. And the brightest memory of her childhood concerned a dress: she always wanted to have her own doll and once when the father bought her a beautiful dress she cut it into pieces and made a doll and a dress for her doll from that new dress. Grandmother finished five classes of the Jewish school—heder—and dropped out to support the family. She started working at 12 years old, making cigarettes, and that was her job until she married at 21.

By that time her parents had died from typhus and soon she was told about her future husband. The young people met and she understood that he was a reliable person: he was not just very tall, handsome and strong, but he had a good skill—shoemaking—and "he knew life". Though he was 25, he was already a widower: his parents arranged his first marriage when he was 16 years old and he had two daughters who had lived with his mother–in–law since their mother (her daughter) died from typhus. Besides, he was an experienced, brave soldier, cavalryman of the picked troops of Czarist Guard. He saw the last Russian Czar, Nicholai II, who asked his guardians in a simple manner: "Hey, guys, does anybody have any complaints?" During 1913–1918 grandfather participated in the Turkish campaign, in World War I, in civil war. Over the years, he used to tell a lot of dramatic, exciting stories of his military career to his children and later to the grandchildren (my son and I know many of them from my husband). And, probably, it was not by chance that in 1941 when the German fascists attacked the U.S.S.R., his son decided voluntarily to become a soldier and to fight like his father against the invaders.

After they married, grandfather worked very hard as a craftsman-shoemaker and grandmother took care of the house and the children. Small and thin, she got the nickname "roach" (a small dried fish). In Vetka where they lived and where the people knew each other, nicknames were customary. This habit of endowing a person with a nickname convinced me, in a sense, once more that the world is really tight and the earth is round. Long ago when I was describing my family to my husband and mentioned that my father's parents lived in Vetka and the father's mother whose name was Doba was so tall that the neighbors called her "Doba lamp-post," he gasped, amazed: "My grandmother when I was a child told me that her parents repeated a story about how Doba-Tower was crossing the brook." No doubt "Tower" was really my grandmother, for she was at least 20 years older than my husband's grandparents and was so tall that it was impossible for her to hide herself in a crowd at the market; she was the tallest woman in the town, strict, serious, sublime, well-shaped, a mother of seven children and a widow rather early in her life. The fact that our grandmothers "met" by chance, in our memories, struck us.

My husband's grandmother told me that nicknames were so popular and ordinary that actually everyone had one. The only person without one (as far as she knew) was a grandfather. His name was Alter and everybody addressed him as Alter. There was one remarkable thing about him: he never tried to adjust to the discomfort and humiliation of the Jews in an anti-Semitic hostile environment, never tried to conceal his background. Wherever and whenever he came, regardless of the rank or educational level of an official or institution, he introduced himself firmly "Hello, I am a Jew from Vetka [and later 'from Gomel']. My name is Alter," and only then started with his subject.

The Jewish people tried to limit the use of Yiddish to their own family or to a narrow circle of a very close friends. They had to "russificate" the Jewish names or conceal their official names by replacing them with the Russian ones, especially, for their children. For example, grandmother's children went by the Russian "Zina", and "Kolya." And I found out the real, official name of my mother-in-law only when we were doing papers for emigrating to the U.S.A. Grandmother herself was called "Anya"; quite by chance I knew that her real name was "Haya." When I asked her about it she answered: "How could I be Haya if Anya is in all their anecdotes about us?" "But Grandfather did not hide his name, he was always Alter, wasn't he?" I asked. And she replied with a quiet smile, "Grandfather? He never hid, never afraid of anything." And she told me the following story, which later my husband retold to me relishing and laughing.

It was several years before grandfather's death. He was sitting in a yard, as usual, at his working place when a respectful neat man came up to him and gave him a pair of shoes to fix. The old man was working and while the stranger was waiting they talked about various things. The grandfather had already finished one shoe and started to repair the other one when suddenly grandmother came out on the porch, approached the shoemaker with a pot of cooked meat and asked him something in Yiddish. The stranger whistled and said in a brash tone, "Ah, you are a Jew, old man! If I knew that you were a Jew I would not have repaired my shoes here." Grandfather froze only for a second. Next moment he took the fixed shoe, jerked the stuck sole and flung the shoes, one by one, far away, on the road. "Go ahead," he said to the shocked stranger, "bring them to a non–Jew."

"Stubborn" (by grandmother's definition), hot-tempered, straight and independent, he resisted anti-Semitic assault as well as other troubles in his life. Only once his spirit seemed to be broken so hopelessly that he even wanted to commit suicide, and grandmother helped him to overcome the heaviest grief, the heaviest news. It was during World War II, in 1942, when they received an official notification that their 18-year-old son was missing in action; his body was not found among alive, wounded or killed soldiers.

The Great Patriotic War embraced the different genera-tions, families in many villages and towns preparing for the victims a common fate—a nightmare of extermination. Those of the Jews who for any reason did not evacuate were literally doomed to death. My mother's grandparents, an old rabbi and his sick wife who lived in Kozelets near Kiev (I mentioned them at the beginning of my essay), were found by the fascists, driven, by foot, to Kiev and buried alive in Babi Yar, together with hundreds of other victims. My grand-mother Doba's daughter (I was named after her) was shot ruthlessly together with her four children, the oldest of them 9 years old and the youngest just 2. The grandfather's two adult daughters from the first marriage perished in a bomb-ing, on their way to find escape in the father's and step-mother's home. Grandmother persuaded him that he should live and evacuate in order to save their last child and to wait for a missing son. Their boy would come back for sure: nobody had seen him dead and, if alive, he would find them.

The days passed, the terrible war was over and they moved from Suchumi (Georgia), where they had spent two years in evacuation, back home, and found only ruins in-stead of their home. Everything was burned out. Grandmother was crying day and night, and this time the old shoemaker supported her, resisting the wish to die. The tragedy and troubles seemed to affirm his trust in God. He visited several secret places where the Jews could gather and pray. On the contrary, grandmother who also was a religious person before the war, lost her trust in God and turned away from religion. "God, if he only existed, would have never allowed this war to happen and take our sons," she said.

She became blind, possibly from the endless tears, from grief. Once she responded, "They [eyes] were sick always [she suffered from an eye disease in the childhood] but they failed when my soul filled with pain."

From all the stories she told me the brightest were those about her beloved son. Strong, tall, handsome, obedient, he was their pride, their greatest success in life. He was a talented self-taught musician; all those towhom he taught music later became professional musicians. He was a good sportsman and an excellent student. He graduated from high school with the gold medal. His record was so eloquent he might have attended military college. He made another choice—to go to the regular army as a soldier-volunteer, though his father wanted him to get a higher education. That was the only time he disobeyed his parents.

In 1965 grandmother and grandfather finally got an apartment which the authorities let them occupy as a family of a perished soldier. In 1985 the officials sent notification that grandmother could come and register for an the installation of a telephone. It was three years after she died.

Her death coincided with the birth of her great-grandson. She predicted his birth, she was waiting for him. The little creature has a full right to know what his roots are on this earth, where he came from, how his great-grandmother, whom he resembles so strikingly, lived, what she liked and what she cried about, what she left in her time and place undone and he, her descendant, might finish, accomplish. She died long ago; my son is 13 today. But it is not too late.

I am opening my eyes, and the train, remote, with its fifth car, disappears slowly. We'll meet it again. We shall fill the gap. We'll sit down, together with our boy, and open the family albums.

I hope his "train" of family linkages one day will be longer than just six cars.

aRkaÒy aminov

I t had never crossed my mind that the time would come when I would have to interview my grandfather from my mother's side about his life. It is a pity that this face-to-face interview could not happen since my grandfather passed away long ago. I've decided to interview my grandfather's sister, who has been living in New York since 1991, because she knows much about his life. I told her about the purpose of the interview, she arranged for the time and this is what I found out about my grandfather's life.

My grandfather, Isaak, was born in Uzbekistan—the country of bright sunny sky, green fields and rich land. He was born in the small town of Kokand on October 5, 1920. It was the third year after the victory of the Great October Revolution in Russia. Back then, Uzbekistan was one of the provinces of the Great Russian Empire.

My grandfather's childhood, teen years and adulthood were spent during the time when the socialist system existed in Uzbekistan and throughout the U.S.S.R. My grandfather was born into the Buckharian-Jewish family of a well-known teacher, Ari, who taught Jewish children native language and literature. It was the time of the middle twenties when there were Jewish schools, Jewish theater, a Jewish paper in the town of Kokand. It was the time when the Communist

121

party allowed the minorities to educate their people in their native languages. Then, at once, everything disappeared. It all began when the laws of the communist government authorized that the Russian and Uzbek languages were to be the official languages in schools and colleges in Uzbekistan. Schools were also allowed to teach some foreign languages, but not Hebrew. The government considered Hebrew an ancient "dead" language and, thus, not to be spoken by anyone whatsoever. The Jewish people were not allowed to go to synagogues. But all these restrictions were not an obstacle for the Jewish people of the town. People never gave up, for they knew that without all this their nation would not survive and be lost forever. The Bukharian-Jewish customs and traditions continued to live among the Bukharian people, and, most of all, the language was never forgotten. The Bukharian language had been spoken among the family members only.

In spite of all that, my grandfather got a basic Jewish education from his father, and he could read religious books in Hebrew. When my grandpa was a little boy, he, just like others, liked to play noisy games and other games such as football (soccer). He spent his childhood through the hardships of the twenties when the civil war in Russia came to an end. During that time children did not have a good childhood, but they always hoped that tomorrow would be better than today.

My grandfather liked to help his mother with her household. He brought water, chopped wood and prepared meals with his mother, for he was the oldest child in the family and he felt responsible for making daily routines easier for his mother, whom he loved very much. In his spare time he liked to read books, especially about breathtaking adventures, and he dreamed of his future. (Who does not dream when one is young and full of hope?) He dreamed of becoming a schoolteacher in chemistry and biology. As a student in high school he liked those subjects and was a "B" student. He wanted to share his knowledge with kids at school, and he wanted to teach them to see the beauty of the world around them. When my grandfather, Isaak, graduated from college and got his diploma, he was ready to accept the responsibilities of a teacher, but he never did. He was 21 years old, and it was the summer of 1941. World War II broke out and he had to leave his home to defend his motherland against Nazi Germany.

He was a soldier for four long years of war and was decorated several times, the most important and memorable being the medal for bravery.

The war was finished for my grandfather when he was badly wounded near the city of Kenigsburg in East Prussia. He spent almost a year in the military hospital and then returned home to Uzbekistan. He remembered the war for the rest of his life. For a long time he experienced nightmares. He could not watch movies about the war, because they reminded him about its horror and the loss of his friends.

In 1945, when my grandfather returned home, he was 25 years old. It was a very difficult postwar time. He had to support his family, so he had to change his profession. He became a bookkeeper and worked at the same firm until he reached the age of 65 and retired.

At the age of 27 my grandfather got married. My grandmother was then 25 years old. They had first met in summer camp when they were children. He was attractive to her because he was handsome, strong and funny to be around. They spent their student years in different places: my grandpa in the town of Fergana and my granny in the town of Samarkand. After the war was over, they met again, got married and had three children—a boy and two girls. My grandparents lived in marriage together for forty-three years, brought up their children, gave them education and saw them married. Later, my grandparents were very happy and proud to see their seven grandchildren growing up.

Through all his life my grandfather nurtured a love of reading. He collected the books written by famous Russian writers such as Dostoyevsky, Sholokhov, Pushkin, and Tolstoy and by foreign writers such as Dumas, Hugo, Arthur Conan Doyle, and Ernest Hemingway. He was also fond of movies and operettas. Since his teen years, soccer was one of his favorite games. As a soccer player himself, he was a good forward and was a member of the student and the town soccer teams. Everybody who watched him play enjoyed his skills. Later he became a big fan of the game.

Time was passing by. My grandparents grew older, and it was my granny who passed away first. My grandpa was left alone and his sister was alone too, for she did not have a family and children. They decided to live together as they once had when they both were children. They were not abandoned though, for grandfather's son and daughters were always at their side physically and spiritually. His sister, who recites this story, recalls that my grandpa missed my granny very much and beseeched God to not let him be too far from his wife and to quicken the unity with her as soon as possible.

Although their spirits might have united, their bodies are and will be in the land where we all were born and lived happily until the summer of 1989, when the bloody riots broke out and our people had to leave, some for Israel and others for the U.S.A., for a better future.

Although I don't have my grandpa anymore, his photographs and the stories told by his younger sister and brother and my own memories about him will always be with me. While these memories are alive, my grandfather will be alive, too.

section iv
economic structure

J ames D. Wolfensohn, president of the World Bank, at a financiers' meeting in Hong Kong, described the state of poverty in the world today. He said that three billion people continue to live on less than $2 a day. Ten percent of the world's population earns 1 percent of the income while the richest 20 percent enjoy over half. He called it "the tragedy of exclusion" (*The Earth Time*, October 1–15, 1997, p. 3). This presents the big picture, so large as to be almost incomprehensible. The description of the lives of some of the grandparents presents the little picture of poverty, on a most personal level. You read about a mother and daughter who went to the dumps to see what they could find, cleaned it at home, and sold it in the market. One grandmother registered her two boys in school, one in the morning, the other in the afternoon, so the two brothers could wear the same pair of shoes. Another grandmother remembers her mother crying at night because she had no food to give to her children.

Often, ethnic groups center around the same occupation. The Chinese have their Chinese restaurants and Chinese laundries, the Greeks have their diners and painting businesses, the Jews have their garment industry, the diamond center, and psychoanalysis, the Koreans have their fruit stores, the Irish became policemen and politicians.

For almost all the students' grandparents, life was a struggle for money, food and lodging. The personal narratives made the students understand what it was like to live in their grandparents' days. A personal vision conveyed the significance and meaning of life behind the economic struggle. One of the most important trends of modern economic systems is the scale of large organizations. Corporations are becoming larger conglomerates and multinational. Some immigrants got jobs as unskilled workers. Others, in the face of large corporations, built their own small family businesses using the investment of a hardworking wife. In these cases family and work became one, unlike the general trend of modern business separating home and work. Such arrangements have their advantages as well as their problems. Long hours in the retail and restaurant business, with limited financial resources, cannot maintain itself unless family members pitch in. But when people at work bring with them personal family relationships, there may be problems. A grandfather who discusses his business with his granddaughter is really giving not only a personal account but a morality narrative. He takes advantage of the attentive granddaughter to deliver a lecture on ethics.

Economic factors are always related to other variables. The grandchildren seldom plan to take over the economic positions of the grandparents. With the opportunity for better education, and with new electronic industries and frontiers of knowledge, the young grandchildren have other aspirations. While the problem of young Americans is how to maintain the economic status of the parents, these students will enjoy upward mobility.

yuet ngor chan

As I was walking happily toward my grandmother's apartment, I could imagine her place full of people. These people were not strangers. They were all my grandmother's children and her grandchildren. Twice a year this little apartment was crowded. This occasion was her seventieth birthday. I believe that there must be hundreds of stories in her life. These stories help tell her history on this earth.

My aunt opened the door. I walked up to my grandmother and wished her a Happy Birthday. If I did not talk with my grandmother very often, I would never know much about her life. Looking at her kind face is what led my thinking back to her life stories.

My grandmother said that children like me are very lucky because they have school to attend. They don't need to worry about many other things. Grandmother remembers that at age 10 in China, she left her family and was sold to someone as a servant. That night was the coldest night. The wind blew very hard. The trees were hitting a window as if telling her, "This is the end of your life." Her body was shaking and hungry at the same time. This period during the war was the worst time of her life. Many days she didn't have rice to eat. If it continued like this, the whole family would die. While she was thinking how bitter her life was, her mother came to her and said, "My dear daughter, you are a big girl now." While she was talking to my grandmother, she gently touched her hair with her hand and expressed her affection and sadness. My grandmother was not sure if her mother's sadness was caused by something specific or life in general. As her mother continued, my grandmother suddenly realized she wanted to give her away. My grandmother didn't feel sad: it was the bitter truth of life. Her mother then said "Anything can happen, my daughter, and you have to be strong. You have to learn to take care of yourself. Don't be afraid to go on in life. Mom loves you, but I don't think I can take care of you."

The next day her mother helped her put on her best clothes and pack the things she needed. Her mother held her hand tightly and then walked away. My grandmother knew what had happened even though her mom didn't tell her that she had been sold to a rich family as a servant. She didn't cry; she kept her words in her heart. When she needed strength, it came from her heart. She told herself that she would take whatever would happen in her life.

Her mom sold her for one hundred and twenty dollars to the rich family when she was 10 years old. She worked seven years for that family. She was lucky because the family treated her well and she only had to do house chores for them. Life was not hard for her in these years. In fact, she learned to be more independent. She grew up stronger for her later life.

Another turning point in her life was when she was 17 and the head of the family died. Then her mother matched her to a man whom she had never met. Of course that man is now my grandfather. She was not very happy when she found out that her husband came from the poorest family in his village. But she didn't feel really bad that she hadn't had a chance to choose her own husband, because it was traditional in China that all marriages were arranged by the parents. A further restriction was that people who had the same last name or lived in the same village could not get married.

Although she was not very pleased about her marriage, my grandmother knew that she was going to stay with that man no matter what.

The shortage of material and food was not the worst thing in her life. The truly grievous experience was that life had no security. In 1953 during the war Japanese planes flew over and looked for people to kill. Life was very unstable—people were crying everywhere for there was not much food left. Dead bodies were found all over the streets. My grandmother was carrying her first baby, my father, and hid in the mountains whenever she heard the planes overhead. "We were lucky not to die then," she said.

I also wanted to ask why she had so many children. In fact, she did not want so many. She is an uneducated person. She doesn't even know how to write. Therefore, she knew nothing about birth control. Whenever she had a baby, she delivered it herself. That's why she had nine children—actually, she had ten. When she gave birth to the tenth child, she didn't give him a chance to live. This was the most hurtful thing in her whole life. She was so guilty and sad. Her heart was breaking. She cried and cried day and night during that time. However, she had no choice. To raise nine children was hard enough. She didn't want things to get even worse. The hardest part of her life was to raise all her children well in a bad situation. They were poor and her children didn't have many clothes, so one outfit was worn for a long time. Sometimes, they fixed a cloth to the point where they did not know which piece was the original one. She could tolerate her children living in a poor environment, but she insisted that they have good values in their lives. To help them develop good personality and behavior, she taught them patiently about life. And she punished them firmly whenever they did something wrong. As a result, they learned to love and share things with one another. The family was very close. It is not easy to raise nine children. My grandmother is really a successful mother.

My grandmother continues her story. Children gradually grew up. Life did not get any better. In 1972, my third uncle went to live in Hong Kong. That was almost the biggest turning point of her life because, after several years, my uncle sent her money making her life much easier. Then thirteen years ago they all—except my family—moved to America. She was so happy and she thanked God for giving her children their own families and better lives in America. She felt she had done her job in her life.

Yuet, what's wrong with you, daydreaming again? Come on, let's sing your grandmother a birthday song. My aunt wakes me up, bringing me back to the present. I am looking at my grandmother's happy face and enjoying the laughter from the children in the joyful apartment. I say to my grandmother in my heart, "Grandmother, enjoy the rest of your life."

elene dramitinos

nitsa is a 41-year-old woman who grew up in Greece and later came to America. She is my mother.

Elene: Going back to your childhood and growing up, what goals did you have?

Nitsa: I was a very depressed child, Elene. I'm sorry to say this, but it's the truth. In our family we weren't very happy. My father was very abusive and my mother struggled to raise us. My grandmother helped my mother to raise us. My mother would then go out and work for other people to try to make us survive. I had no goals.

E: Did you enjoying doing anything? -

N: I used to enjoy singing. I used to sing as a child. Unfortunately, I smoke now and my voice is gone. But I always used to say to my mother I wanted to become a singer.

E: Did you consider it more like a dream, then, wanting to pursue it as a goal in life?

N: Yes, everybody has dreams, but I never dreamt of coming to America.

E: Why did you get married at the age of 14?

N: Back then in Greece, setup marriages were very common. After my father died, my mother could not support the whole family anymore. Your father was brought to my house by my uncle to choose one of my sisters, but your father chose me instead. I was to marry your father a few months later.

E: How did you feel toward your mother? She was telling you that you had to marry a man you had never met beforehand and did not love at first. Did you hate her?

N: No, I was very young and scared. I went and hid with the chickens. People were looking for me and I didn't want to see anybody. Then, later on, my mother said, "There is a very good man, a handsome man, who's looking to get married and wants to marry you. We need someone to support the family."

E: So the motives for your marriage were to support the family and for my father to have a wife?

N: Yes, your father came along, had a few dollars in his pocket and the idea that he came from America made people think he was a very rich and important person. Greek people think that America is where easy money is made and the streets are paved with gold. So, basically, I got married to save the family. My father died and the only thing my mother had was the house and us girls to support. After my father died, people started to come around asking for the money that my father owed them. My father owed a lot of money to a lot of people. People, though, were afraid of my father because he was 6 foot 4 inches and very strong. Nobody would even dare to look at him, so when he died people started to threaten my mother about taking our house.

E: Are you okay, Mom?

N: Yes, Elene, I'm fine. Let's continue with this.

E: Continue with the process of the marriage setup, in brief?

N: I was engaged for two weeks and was married in my mother's village, Roufa. I was nervous through the whole wedding and the affair afterwards. I did not speak much at all. A month later I was on my way to America, your father and I.

E: What did you think America would be like?

N: I didn't know, Elene. I was just a little kid. I was very scared. America seemed like a dream, a castle and something you can't imagine. I don't know. I can't describe how I felt.

E: Did you think America was going to be an escape?

N: I thought America was going to be great. Everything was going to be O.K., but it wasn't the way I thought at all.

E: What do you mean?

N: I came here and I had no family, no friends and I did not know anything about America. I felt lost and like I had gone to another planet or something.

E: What is the first thing you remember when you came to America?

N: The first thing I remember is the airport and the lights flying down. It seemed as if it would never end and I was totally lost and fell asleep in your father's lap on the way home. I couldn't stand the lights. Elene, before I married your father I was never out of the village. I was born and raised in a small village on an island in Crete. We had no electricity, we didn't even have toilet paper. No bathrooms, we used to go out in the fields. All of sudden you leave a small village and you go into NYC and there is a big difference.

E: Where did he bring you after you left the airport?

N: He had rented an apartment in Queens Village. We had one couch that turned into a bed, one table, two forks, spoons and plates.

E: How would you describe the early years in America?

N: Your father went to work in his brother's restaurant in NYC, working fourteen hours a day. I used to stay home alone and didn't do much because I didn't know much yet. In a matter of eight months I had lost thirty pounds. I had no family and your father's family really didn't bother with me or spend time with me.

E: Did you keep contact with your family in Greece?

N: Yes, once in a while I would talk to my family in Greece. Along with a letter I would also send my mother some money. But I missed them very much.

E: Did you want to leave America?

N: Yes, I wanted to go back and see my family. Then your father started taking me to work with him because I had fallen into a deep depression. I would not talk or eat and had no energy for anything. Your father thought I was going crazy and in my own way I was. When your father started taking me to work, even though I was working long hours, I enjoyed being out of the house. It was there I started to meet people and experience the way of life in America.

E: How did you learn English?

N: I learned English through people. In a restaurant first you learn eggs, bread and butter. Then you learn fried, over or scrambled. Then you start to communicate with people with basic hello and how are you? Even today I still see people who helped me with learning English. I used to say to the customer for example "We have today corned beef and garbage and they would be like, "No, no, it's corned beef and cabbage." Through this I learned English, then later on I went to school. TV was also a big help.

E: Did you learn how to drive?

N: After my first child it was more of a necessity than the idea of just learning to drive. Your father did not want me to have too much freedom or knowledge of American life.

E: On lighter subjects such as music, did you enjoy American music?

N: I loved and still love American music better than Greek music. Greek music is too depressing and always about something sad.

E: Did you wear the bell bottoms?

N: Yes, I did. I also wore the miniskirts, platform shoes and high-collared shirts. I did the whole '70s look. It was one of the major changes for me. In America all types of clothes were here, some were cheap and some were so expensive. When I first arrived I settled for whatever your father gave me, but later on I had my own style of clothing I liked to wear.

E: So when did you start to like America and accept it as your home?

N: Elene, when I first came to America, life here was very hard. I was very lonely and sad. What I am today and what I have, I had to work very hard for. Your father and I worked fourteen hours each day in your uncle's restaurant until we saved enough money to open a place of our own. Nothing was given to me or your father easily. Eventually, we bought a house in Queens Village when the area was nicer. George and you were eventually born and that really brought me joy and love. I think it wasn't till you and George were born that I accepted America as my home.

Even though my mother would visit me here and eventually my sister came to America, I still hadn't accepted America as my home. I love you and George very much, and where you and George are I am too.

E: I love you too Mom.

E: Getting back to when you first arrived in America. What was your first experience at one of America's favorite fast food franchise's, McDonald's?

N: You know I really don't like fast foods. The only thing I really remember is that I took you and George there a lot as little kids to eat and that twenty years ago the french fries were five cents.

E: Did you visit all the famous places such as the Statue of Liberty, Empire State Building, etc.?

N: The only times I really ever went to those places were when someone either from your father's side or my side came from Greece to visit us. I never really had much time to see NYC. I still would like to do a lot of things in the city that I haven't had the opportunity to see. I would like one day to see a Broadway show.

E: I'll take you one day.

E: How many years have you been living in America?

N: It's about thirty years now that I have been in America.

E: Do you feel more like an American or a Greek?

N: I can't answer that question in the sense of how you are asking it. I love being both but sometimes I don't know which one I am. I was born in Greece but I grew up in America. America has been my home for almost thirty years now. I love America. It's given me so much out of life, good and bad. Greece, though, is where I came from, where I was born. I feel like I am stuck between two cultures. Certain aspects of my Greek culture I agree with and some I don't but the same goes for the American culture. I like the fact that I am both and not just one. Sadly, though, Elene, because I left my country at such a young age I never got a chance to learn things about my own country that I was born in. I hear people say things about Greece that I never knew before. The same goes for America. I know very little about America. I still remember a lot of the customs and traditions that I grew up with in Greece. I love both America and Greece.

E: You know, even though I was born in America, when I visit Greece I feel as if my heart belongs there rather than in America. I guess it's your heart which tells you who you are more than geography.

E: Mom, what is your goal?

N: I'm 41 years old. George and you have both grown up now and your father died thirteen years ago. I always worked hard in my life and raised my kids the best I knew how. I feel I never really got to enjoy life. I don't even think I had a childhood; I was married and had kids before I was 21. I would like to be able to live six months in Greece and six months in America. I would like also to enjoy my kids and grandchildren. In a way, I want to be a hippie, wear ripped jeans and travel around the world. I would like to go and visit my own country that I never really had a chance to see before I left. Greece is one of the most beautiful countries. That's my goal, Elene, to be free and enjoy life.

auδRey Gonzales

José Antonio Olavarria was born on January 7, 1900, in a small country in the mountains of San José de Ocoa in the Dominican Republic. He is the eldest son of immigrants from Spain. Altogether my grandparents' parents had six children. There were five boys and one girl. Today there are only two boys alive and he's one of them. During the years that his parents were alive, they were considered to be a wealthy family because they owned plenty of land. But they weren't "rich" because their house was made out of wood with coconut leaves as a rooftop. The boys also had to dedicate their young lives to cultivating their parents' land instead of getting an education. My grandfather never attended school and is therefore illiterate.

But not only did they own land, they owned a lot of cows, sheep, pigs and chickens. On the land they produced plenty of beans, rice, avocado, mango, oranges and plantains. Their richest crop was coffee. They grew enough to feed themselves as well as to trade and sell. Coffee enabled them to buy clothes, condiments to cook and gas for electricity. Money wasn't their source of power, land was—and what they grew on it.

My grandfather spent most of his childhood working. A typical day for him was to get up early in the morning, put on his working clothes and go off to work. When he finished his job for the day, he would go to the river and bathe. They didn't have a bathtub, so they either went to the river or they got buckets of water and bathed in the back of the house. He would bring home a chicken and some rice which his mother and sister cooked for the family dinner. They used carbon because they didn't have a stove.

My grandfather's routine didn't change much, not even after he met my grandmother. She was the daughter of his neighbors and was only 20 years old when they met. My grandfather was 41 years old. Shortly after they began dating, they fell in love and were united but never married. Once they were living together, they began to have children. They had fifteen children in total but only nine survived, five boys and four girls, including my mother. He was still living in the same place where he was born, but after having four children they decided to move to town. He feared that he would get involved in the small wars that the countrymen fought against one another for land. Many of them hid in caves, fearing they would be killed. So in 1966, my grandfather and his family moved to a small town in San José de Ocoa, into a small wooden house. My mom was 14 years old.

The move to town became very difficult because they were raising nine children. It was better because they could go to school, but it was difficult because there were so many mouths to feed and not enough food. So life became a nightmare for my grandfather. Without an education he had to find odd jobs to support his family. His sons had to go out and look for work. Their way of living changed completely for the worse. The children hardly ever went to school, and only one girl out of nine children graduated high school, the youngest one. The family was falling apart, and they needed food and clothes but couldn't afford them. Other family members who were wealthier and living comfortably wanted to give my grandfather a hand. The family was separated and three girls, including my mother, were sent to live with different aunts and uncles. The girls were taken in to be their housekeepers. My grandfather had tried but his luck quickly ran out.

As the years went by and my grandfather aged, the children who had lived with him left to make their own families. My grandparents were left alone in their little wooden house. All his daughters came to the United States for a better life, but he refused to come here because he was already old and he loved his own country. He wouldn't be able to live the "American" life. He preferred his small town where everyone knew one another and there wasn't a lot of noise such as there was in the capital, Santo Domingo.

Today, my grandfather still lives in the same house with my grandmother who is 76 years old. In 1983 my parents helped build a new house out of cement. My grandfather is going to be 98 years old and has never been diagnosed with anything serious. The most he's had is a common cold and he still has all his senses. He has never worn glasses and has almost perfect vision. He is said to be in such great shape because he is the town's "newspaper." He wakes up every morning at five, rain or shine, and runs around town finding out the gossip for the day. The only problem is that he doesn't have any teeth, so it's a little difficult to understand him. He refuses to wear false teeth. What can we do?

My grandfather did the best that he could to raise his children, but it can get very difficult when you are uneducated. Maybe if he had gone to school, his family wouldn't have been separated. But he needed to support his family and he did what he thought was best. His daughters are not upset with him because they had to live with other family members; actually, they are glad. They got an opportunity to better themselves and come to the United States. Now they all send my grandparents money so they can eat well and clothe themselves better. My grandfather also has his other children living in the same town. He is a great father, grandfather, and great-grandfather. He has, altogether, about forty-five grandchildren and ten great-grandchildren. May he continue to live a long and healthy life.

JUDY REYES

People spend their whole lives trying to figure out who they are. They search for answers to questions like "Where did my family originate?" Grandparents and parents have the answers to questions such as this one. When you search for these answers, you find out about the people you call family. It is easy to label a person mom or dad, grandma or grandpa, but you never know what or who they really are. You call them this because you have been taught to. People never take the time to find out about their family history, and before you know it the keepers of the history are gone and the traditions and the stories fade. Sitting with my grandmother and talking about our family made me feel like I knew almost nothing about who I was. I knew the simple things about our family, but she filled in what I was missing, the reasons why she is who she is to me. One Sunday my grandmother and I sat down for two hours, recapping almost fifty years of her life.

My grandmother Felicita grew up in a small village in Puerto Rico named Cuamo. It was mostly farmland and about an hour away from the main town. The town was composed of mostly poor farmers looking to sell their crops to store merchants in town. Every week a truck would pass and pay these farmers for the crops they wanted to sell. Her father worked in town doing odd jobs and her mother stayed home tending to their four children. Her mother taught all the children to read and write. The girls were taught how to sew, crochet, knit and cook. When the girls became good at their crocheting and knitting, they would sell some of their pieces to stores in town.

At the age of 17 my grandmother got a job at a shop doing piece work and tailoring. There she met a man of 21 who worked a pressing machine at the back of the store. It turned out that he lived just down the block from where she did. They became friends and the relationship turned into a romance. Within a year they were married. They rented a shack five blocks away from where her parents lived. The shack had four rooms and was circular in shape. She became pregnant at the age of 19. He kept his job at the shop and she stayed home to take care of the child. They grew their own crops behind the home. As the years progressed, more children came into the house, a total of eight. As they became older they were taught how to tend to the crops. The children were sent to the local school and did chores when they came home.

In the 1960s the economy in Puerto Rico was poor. The family struggled from day to day to survive. Grandpa decided to take a risk and come to the United States to seek a better opportunity for the family. The plan was for him to come first and the family to follow when things were stable. He borrowed from friends to make the trip. It was three years later when the next family member would follow. Little by little the family became reunited. Grandma was the last to come along with the three eldest children.

Their first apartment was in the Williamsburg section of Brooklyn. It was a small two-bedroom apartment with running water inside, something they weren't used to. Back home the water came from a well in the backyard. By this time only five people were still living in the house. The three oldest children moved out on their own. Grandpa was working a factory job doing the same as back home, using a press machine. The conditions were unsanitary. All the fumes of the chemicals used took their toll on him over the years. He couldn't get a better job because his educational level didn't go beyond the eighth grade. When he was young he had to leave school to support his family. Fifteen years and nine grandchildren later he passed on. The family pulled together to support grandma because she was still raising the two youngest children. Her inner strength comes from her children who helped her get over the death.

The most tragic of all events in her life was the passing of her eldest child. A mother always hopes that she never suffers the loss of a child. In 1987 her eldest child died from a boat accident. She fell into a deep depression that she thought she would never recover from. Grandma was always in and out of hospitals. If it wasn't for her children she would not have recovered. They gave her the strength to come back.

These days she talks to the grandchildren about grandpa and my uncle so that we may never forget them. Her famous saying is "you don't know how easy you have it." There are times when she thinks of going back home to Puerto Rico to live. She visits occasionally and goes to see the place she called home, the little shack.

Recapping this part of our family history with grandma let me understand my dad better. My dad does and says things that I never understood. Without knowledge of family history you lose insight on the people you call family.

ANGELICA AGUILAR

I would like this essay to focus on my grandparents' most cherished dream and how little by little, piece by piece, they ended up making it come true through the years. But I must begin by providing some background on their lives.

They were both raised by very poor but honest and hardworking mothers. Both went unrecognized by their fathers. Both came from oversized families, meaning they both had seven or eight brothers and sisters.

They lived closely, in extremely small and cold towns, located three hours from the capital and just minutes away from each other. These towns do not even appear on a regional map of their country of origin, Colombia.

It all started in January 1950. My grandfather, Segundo, met my grandmother, Emma, while assisting at a dance in the plaza of Mongua, my grandmother's town.

Two months later, they got married in my grandfather's town, my grandma not having obtained her mother's permission to do so. They sealed their wedding at four o'clock in the morning, since they had an unwritten contract with the owner of a hacienda (farmhouse). It was there that they agreed to start working at six in the morning of that same Sunday.

They were both very young at that time. My grandfather was 21 years old and his bride only 14. She cooked for a dozen workers and helped with the cleaning of the house, while he was employed in the fields. They worked like slaves and the wages were reduced because the owner charged them for the food and the small room they slept in.

After a year they moved to another hacienda. The conditions remained the same. Then my grandmother gave birth to their first son, Juan. They did not last long at this place and soon the three of them moved to another hacienda. Still they were mistreated, were paid little wages and the farm work was even more exhausting.

It was then that they started getting more obsessed with their dream of having their own house and a better life. After they had lived for three years in haciendas, luck finally struck and grandpa got a job working as a policeman in a town called Belencito.

They moved there, and after six years of saving every single peso, they had enough money to buy a medium piece of field, on which they could construct their own home in Bogotá (the capital). It was a big opportunity, in fact, the break of a lifetime.

The housing was created on the basis of a special program, called *alianza para progreso* (Alliance for Progress), brought into being by U.S. President John F. Kennedy in the early 1960s to help South American nations overcome poverty.

After a while, my grandfather transferred to another police station in Bogotá. Those were really hard times too, since they did not know anybody in such a big city and had many expenses.

By then, they already had three more children: Nohora, Luis (my dad) and Manuel. My grandfather worked all day and at night he pursued high school studies "by mail." Then he went to SENA, a technical school. After three years he got a degree as a telecommunications technician. He then got a better job working at an airport.

While working at the airport, he initiated the construction of the back part of the house, which included three new bedrooms, a bathroom and the enlargement of the living room.

Three years later, my grandfather got a job related to his degree, working at a communications corporation. He then started the construction of a second floor, including two bedrooms, a living room, kitchen and bathroom in the front section and three rooms with a bathroom in the rear, as well as a terrace. By then all their seven children had been born. They all got married at very young ages too.

Every time one of their sons or daughters was married, the bridal couple came to live at my grandparents' house, the place where the family had lived their entire lives. It was like a ritual. They lived there all together, and after five or six years each couple had accumulated enough money to buy their own house and move out.

On weekends, all of us got together at my grandparents' huge place, visiting *los viejos*, (old-parents). We danced, made BBQs on the terrace, told stories and sometimes jokes. I grew up playing and fighting with all my twenty-eight cousins at least two weekends each month. We must have celebrated at least thirty-five Christmas dinners and had more than a hundred birthday parties.

After thirty-three years, my grandparents decided to sell the house. Their decision affected all of my close family in a profound way. By then, I was already living in this country. According to my *viejos*, they felt they had no choice since the neighborhood (named Kennedy after the U.S. President) had in less than a year become very dangerous with drugs sold on every corner.

To this day, four years after the selling, I still have in my mind the clear picture of staying over at my grandparents' dream house on weekends. In my memory there remain stories of how hard they worked to offer their children their own place to live.

They taught us that family must stick together through all times. They made all of us try our best in getting along with one another. And most importantly, they taught us how, in order to succeed in life and make our dreams a reality, we had to work hard—even if it took a lifetime.

ekaterini kokkali

I came to America almost nine months ago and I live with my grandfather on my mother's side. Therefore, I got a face-to-face interview with him. My grandfather is a tall, dark-skinned man with still dark hair (but not black anymore) and a gray mustache. He is 82 years old now and was born on December 15, 1915. He originally came from Greece and is named Antonios Frousios.

In his family there were six children. Anto was the third child and the only boy in the family. Having a male child was very appreciated in the Greek mentality, and that is why Anto was spoiled. In addition, Anto's father was the richest man in Thiva, so Anto thought he could do and get whatever he wanted. That fact made him overreact a few times. For example, when Anto was seventeen years old he wanted a fast horse with which he could run faster than the train itself. When his father refused to buy him the horse, trying to protect him, Anto went up on the roof of his home and started to scream that he was going to kill himself if he did not get the horse he was dreaming of because without the horse his life would be meaningless. The objective was to get the horse.

At the age of 24, Anto overreacted once again when he threatened to kill the family of Eleftheria (the girl whom he

had fallen in love with at the first sight) by pouring petro-
leum around the house and lighting it with a match if her
mother kept preventing them from being together. His
threats resulted in his getting what he wanted, Eleftheria.
They finally got married in December 1941 in Anto's house
(World War II had started and the Nazis didn't allow
churches to be open). After the ceremony was over, Anto
went back to fight against the Nazis. Eleftheria and Anto had
three children, two daughters and a son. Anto's weak spot
was always his middle child, Stella, and he raised her as a
boy.

Sixteen years after his marriage, Anto's father died.
Without him, Anto was lost. He took over the property and
the cash but he did not know how to handle money. He only
knew how to spend it by hanging out or helping friends and
relatives. After a couple of years, Anto's wife became seriously ill from an unexplained and unknown illness. Anto
spent the last of his money on doctors in a successful effort
to save his wife's life.

Anto's oldest sister was at that time an immigrant in
America and invited him to go there. The whole procedure
allowing Anto and his family to imigrate to America took
two years. Meanwhile he had moved with his family to
Athens. He opened a grocery shop and when he saved all
the money he needed for the trip, he left with his wife and
their youngest child, then an 8-year-old boy. Their daughters
did not accompany them because the invitation from his
sister left out their names. Eleftheria and Anto were supposed to invite them from America. In October 1968, Anto
with his wife and son made the trip on a boat which lasted
almost a month. He refused to talk to me about the conditions of traveling, but he told me his worst experience was
seeing his wife worried about their two girls they had left
behind. He said, "Nina (the way they call me in my family—

it comes from my name but it sounds more like a love term), that was when I realized how wonderful a mother is. I am absolutely sure that if your grandmother had the money instead of me, we would still be in Greece. You see, when I was spending my money around I wasn't thinking about my children. I was so selfish to think that the money was only mine and I could do whatever I wanted with it. But a mother is almost never selfish. She just gives and, most of the time, considers her children before she does anything."

When they first came to America they stayed at Anto's sister's house. At the beginning he worked in a bar, cleaning it during the night. Eleftheria worked as a finisher in a fur market. Anto was making only seventy dollars a week, but Eleftheria, because she was good at her job and fast, was earning much more. After two years in America, she gave him six thousand dollars to open a restaurant. It was half Greek traditional foods and half fast food, serving hot dogs, hamburgers and sandwiches. They had their first restaurant in 1970, on 44th Street and Sixth Avenue in New York City. Two years later they opened one in New Jersey.

Anto did not know a word of English, so he hired staff who knew English either because they were born and raised in America or had come here to study. He advertised in the newspaper and hired people from the neighborhood who were in need of jobs. After a while, Anto bought a private house. During this time his oldest daughter got married. According to Greek tradition, a father should give something to his son-in-law as a present after the marriage. It is the way to show him that from now on you consider him a member of your family and you love him like one of your own. My grandfather, with this mentality, put his son-in-law's name on the contracts for one of the restaurants and the house. After a few years his daughter got divorced and his son-in-law took the one restaurant in order to cancel his rights on the family house.

In 1980 a real estate company bought the other restaurant from my grandfather for twenty-three thousand dollars. Anto was already 65 years old and retired. His wife, who was 8 years younger, continued working as a finisher in a fur market while Anto kept busy with the chores at home.

All these events are more or less the most important ones in my grandfather's 82 years of life. To my last question, which was, "What would you change from what you did or did not do, if you could turn back time?" he responded, "Well, Nina, two things I would never do again. First, I would never spend my money without thinking about my children. I would become a good, responsible father sooner. And secondly, I would never ever again put my son-in-law's or daughter-in-law's name on my property contracts as presents. And do you know why, Nina mou [my Nina]? Because no one else would ever love your children as much as you do. And even if they are lucky enough to find someone to love them that powerfully, you can never be absolutely sure about it. Nobody will give you guarantees and one of your roles as a parent is to always protect your children from unpleasant surprises, at least from the ones that you can.

"Keep two things always in mind, be careful regarding everything you do that can affect the people you care about and learn how to deal with money, because things in life do not always stay the same. Give your children the best that you can, protect them from anything that can harm them, if possible, but make them tough. Life is not easy at all. Teach them self-confidence, the importance of money, the value of family and the trust in friendship. Teach them how to be selfish but only to a point and to always think about the people who are really important to them."

"Give them everything you can, but be rough with them, do not spoil them, it is the worst thing you can do to them and you do not want to harm them, do you? Of course not, that is why you should do what I told you and something more. Teach them to have trust in other people but without trusting them blindly. People very often in this life are not exactly what they pretend to be. Friends you thought you knew are not always real friends, and relatives you loved are not always there for you as you were for them. I've said already too much and I do not want to say anything else, besides, I get tired, but teach them to have both of their feet on the ground. That is the best thing you can do for them."

While I was walking away from him, he called me once more to tell me, "I am an old man, life has many situations and hides many things that probably I would not be there to advise you on. That is why you should do me a favor, will you? All these things that I told you before keep them as a big and valuable charm and treasure them not only for your future children but for guiding you as well. Take my advice and you won't lose. By doing that you will be the best example for your children as well as I was for mine and try not to repeat my huge mistakes."

After the interview was over I realized for the first time in my life why my mother was always so tough on me, even though I am the only kid in my family. All this time I was wondering how it was possible that my father spoiled me and not my mother. I recalled all the times she was rough on me about something. Late that night I called her to thank her. She was touched by that action and admitted that in many situations she was sure that I was going to do the right thing, but she was determined to protect me from any mistake that I could avoid, and in order to do that she had to be tough. I asked, "Why is daddy so different than you, though?" She replied, "Nina mou, your daddy has no reason to be different than he is right now. Do not forget he comes from a very controlling family, especially with money and property. To him the control with money is second nature and he considers it an inborn instinct, but I know it's not exactly like this." She was so right. I have caught myself a few times, now that I'm so far from her, spending my money on phone cards in order to talk to her. Most of the time she yelled at me on the phone not to call her again for a least one or two days and I thought she hadn't missed me at all. Now I know how right she was. There are times when the money you spend today would cover a need you'll have tomorrow.

The following day I walked down to 44th Street and Sixth Avenue after my classes were over and found on this corner a bank named Fleet Bank and, above the bank, the Murray Hill Properties (Managing Agent), a building of twenty-one floors. I stared at that corner a few minutes and I recalled my grandfather's and mother's words. I really believe now that this interview was helpful and good for me. It brought me closer to my family's past and made me understand things that before seemed absolutely unexplained.

BENJAMIN ANDREWS

m y grandmother, Mrs. Lydia King, was born in Trinidad in August of 1927. She was the fourth born out of six; she has four brothers and a sister. As she was growing up the only grandparents she knew were her mother's parents. She lived close to school but only went until she was around 10 because she got a foot injury and stopped going. She went to an Anglican church almost every Sunday for Sunday school and regular Mass.

The popular foods during that time were pelau (rice and peas), fish broth, stew, chicken, beef, pork and rice provision, which was white yam, cassava, sweet potato, dasheen, plantain, edos, carrots, white potato and breadfruit. This was widely eaten and got the name provision because all the ingredients were roots and vegetables that came from your own garden. Breakfast consisted of farina, which is dry grated cassava that can be made into a porridge if heated with milk or water, a popular snack was channa (dried and seasoned chick peas) and tamarind, a sour fruit coated with sugar for a sweet and sour flavor, and mangoes (a very common fruit).

The way people survived when my grandmother was growing up was if you were well off and had a good and prosperous garden, you gave to the people who didn't. The people in your neighborhood looked out for you and you looked out for them. Everyone helped one another so you could all survive. Most people also had their own chicken coop which provided eggs that were sometimes sold at the market. Hustling on the streets of Trinidad's capital Port of Spain was another way to provide money to live.

My grandmother grew up at a time when Trinidad was underdeveloped. When she was young there were very few cars and most of the roads were unlit. Most of the country had a rural environment filled with dirt roads and dense forests. The country was in the process of having roads and buildings built. The houses of the poor of that time were built out of either straw or dirt; those who could afford it used wooden boards and bricks.

At that time Americans did most of the masonry and construction work in building Trinidad. Americans helped to quickly develop Trinidad by paving and putting up street lights on the roads. They also built many buildings and dug wells to provide clean water with ease. As the 1 940s began, buses and cabs filled the streets, cars were popular and World War II was just about to get under way. My grand-mother remembers that a lot of the older males joined the navy to fight under Great Britain since Trinidad was then a British colony.

During World War II my grandmother and other Trinidadians felt the effect of the war just like any U.S. citizen. All items like rice, sugar, milk, beef, etc., had to be rationed. A card had to be shown to receive food. British ships often passed by the capital of Tobago, Scarborough, then went to Port of Spain (Trinidad's capital) during the war. In her late teenage years she would hang out at the wharf where all of the British and American soldiers' boats would dock. There people would relax and listen to tunes from a gramophone (record player) and from organs (the music that Trinidad is famous for, calypso and steelband music, became popular in the '50s).

After the war my grandmother had her first child at age 19 and let her grandparents take care of him. She got her first job at 20 doing housework and cleaning. After that job she also worked for the city council doing office work and sidewalk, bush, and street cleaning. She got married in the mid '60s and then in 1969 she came up to America for a better life and the opportunity to get a job. She was sponsored by someone she worked for as a cook. She worked in Venezuela and Chicago and then came to New York. I asked her, "When you came to America was it as prosperous as many immigrants at the time felt it was." She replied, "When I came up it was easier to get a job than it was in Trinidad and things were really inexpensive, for instance, fifteen cents for a bag of rice, twenty-five cents for a train ride and fifteen scents for a bus ride. But the salary that was worked for was very small."

In time she bought a house in Queens and then moved to Philadelphia, where she lives now.

section v
political systems

he function of the political institution is to protect the group from inside and outside aggression, to maintain law and order. The political institution creates the law and enforces the law. It has a monopoly on force.

The nation–state political organization is a fairly new historical form of government, a consolidation of large and small nations entitled to their own territory and sovereignty. The national idea served mainly to create larger units out of fragments of units, like India and Pakistan in place of small ones, but small states like Czechoslovakia and Israel followed. Historians and political scientists suggest that these changes were brought about by the railroad, steamship and telegraph, which made the communication of ideas, exchange of goods and movement of people easier than ever before. These changes advanced the principle of nation-state (*A History of the Modern World*, R. R. Palmer and Joel Colton, Alfred A. Knopf, New York, 1965, p. 511). The concept of nation–state assumes that the people who live in the states are members of a nation under their own supreme authority and their own government and speak the official language of that country. Outsiders are "foreign." A nation may have a shared history, emotional memory and also a shared destiny.

To the degree that the nation–state sees itself responsible for its citizens, it may be thought of as a large community. The states imply geographical principles, of preexisting smaller states united under the political territory, and social psychological principles, which involve a sense of identity and loyalty of citizens to their state. Within this context, immigration is examined as a political movement with social-psychological motivations and consequences.

In many interviews the political institution did not protect the people—quite to the contrary, it deprived them of their basic human rights, sometimes of their lives. Political oppression was often the reason for migration, often taken at a great risk. Illegal immigrants have become part of the daily news and a political issue with continuous stories of people from China, Haiti, Cuba and Mexico who risk their lives and life savings to reach our shores. Many do not make it. Such stories highlight the sense of purpose, the goals and what the American dream means to them. In our early American history Patrick Henry's "Give me liberty or give me death!" sounds sentimental or corny, but when we read some of the stories from China, it sounds real. People did just that: risked their lives for freedom.

If the railway and telegraph brought about the principle of nation-state, the advance communication network enhanced the ideas of individual freedom and civil rights. Behind this notion is the idea of the Declaration of Independence of the unalienable right of "all men" to life, liberty, and the pursuit of happiness. Indeed the purpose of the government is to protect these rights as well as the individual rights to property. This political philosophy is based on that of the English philosopher, John Locke (1632–1704), for whom the government was a contract between the people and their government. Governments are created to protect the individual against harm and denial of rights.

Just as we can say that all the papers can be part of the chapter on the family, so we may argue that every paper is a political statement. Immigration is a political act and many grandfathers remember political upheavals which forced them to flee their country without their property. Property is a political concept: the government may protect it or may take it away. The laws of the land under which some of the grandparents lived are political.

An American student tells about her grandfather who became a military judge in Korea. A local peasant accused of being a communist was sent to prison and the American judge, a lawyer at home in New York, practiced basic principles of democracy and set the prisoner free. Governments cannot control thoughts, but can they control birth rate? Can they punish a citizen for having more children than the government allows? Even those who agree that population explosion is one of the major dangers of the future will question the right of the government to punish families who choose to have more children.

The horrors of war in Europe and the Far East are remembered vividly, a testimony of human cruelty as well as human resiliency and strength. Political orders are linked to compulsory education, to health systems, to family law and every aspect of our lives. Here they are reflected as part of the individual's experience and one's power to act upon them.

kathleen yee

hanksgiving 1981. We had just finished dinner and were sitting in our living room awaiting dessert. Soon, there was a wide variety of desserts as well as conversations floating around the room, some in English, some in Chinese. Above the din, I recall hearing my grandmother's story about the stray cat that followed her home one day in 1955. It was a sweet and funny story of how she toilet-trained it and how my jealous Uncle John threw it out of their four-story window one day only to find out that it had survived, returned and "peed in his bed" that evening. I also learned that my grandmother never named it for she felt cats were too independent to be named and thus considered one's possession—and she was right: two or three years later, the cat walked out the door and never returned to the neighborhood. However, in the interim, she called it "Cat" ("Mew" in Chinese) and fed it fresh liver, never cat food, which she bought from the butcher every week. Somehow, this simple story has remained with me since that evening. It has had an unusual significance for me because it reveals the complete woman that was my grandmother, and also because it was the last Thanksgiving that we spent together, although that was unbeknownst to me at the time.

Christmas came and went without exception. The next occasion was Chinese New Year, which in my family represents for the adults an excuse for yet another family gathering and for the children's receiving money in red envelopes from older, married relatives. Otherwise, we never partook in any of the traditional activities that signified the holiday. On this occasion, my grandmother informed the rest of the family of my childhood antics. I also remember my grandfather saying "crazy kid" several times to sum me up and the times I spent with them. This was the most memorable Chinese New Year for me because I remember anticipating more gatherings and, thus, more stories to come, but that was not to happen, for that summer my family and I moved to California. When I returned a year later for college, my grandmother was treating me like an adult, asking about my goals, my job and other things which were of a more serious nature. The only times we reverted to our former relationship were when I told her about my new cat, Luther, and asked about the story of Mew again and again. She never tired of my numerous requests to hear about her cat, probably because I was the only one who took an interest and because I kept her up on all of Luther's developments.

Unfortunately, these were telephone conversations, held when she called to invite me over for lunch or just a visit. I always politely declined, using either school or work as an excuse because I did not want to face the new nature of the relationship. I knew our days of going to the park and feeding the pigeons were gone as were the annual excursions to 34th Street for the Thanksgiving parade. No more solid chocolate turkeys, Santas, Easter bunnies or red pistachios. No more dolls for Christmas. It never occurred to me that the relationship or either of us would ever age. By 1983, I was 17 and she was 79. While I demanded of my parents to be treated as an adult, I absolutely refused it of my grand-parents, although initially they were more willing to comply than my parents.

Thanksgiving that year was not the same. My parents were conspicuously absent as Thanksgiving had always been held at our house and my grandmother was home with the flu. The year after (1984) my grandfather was hospital-ized in October and they both missed Thanksgiving dinner because my grandmother did not want to leave him alone. By next Thanksgiving, they were both dead.

Thanksgiving 1987. My parents had moved back to New York earlier in the year and we were sitting in my aunt's house. This year there were some new faces: my cousin had returned from Europe with his medical degree and his wife, who had had a baby earlier in the year. Also in attendance was my other cousin's son, Justin. It occurred to me that my grandparents never met these two great-grandchildren of theirs. There were stories about childhood antics, but this time they weren't about me. They were about this new generation of children. Having been assigned to write a biography of a grandparent, my grandmother and her cat story immediately came to mind. She seemed to be the perfect subject because I had known her all my life and had spent a good deal of time with her. It had always been easy to talk with her, so I had some knowledge of the type of person she was. And besides, I wanted to find out more about her youth, of which she almost never spoke. Although she had died two years before, I did not think that would be a deterrence, for there were still surviving relatives who I thought would provide enough information to enable me to piece her life together. What I could not foresee was their lack of information, recall, and at times, cooperation. Fur-thermore, my relatives are dispersed throughout the world, and naturally there is the language barrier since there are different stages of immigration and assimilation within the family. These people run the gamut from sixth-generation distant cousins to newly arrived in-laws. Nevertheless, I persisted and found that even those who were initially cooperative were beginning to admit anything just to cut the conversation short, which resulted in two major problems for me. One was sorting out the lies from the facts, for I realized that some of the statements made in later conversations with my relatives were contradicting their earlier ones. I then faced the challenge of trying to convince them of the importance of the project. It was not merely a matter of a good grade; creative lying could easily achieve that. Rather, it was more a matter of digging up old memories that had been buried long ago. Although most of them wanted to forget their supposedly dismal past, there were those who did not live through it and wanted to know how those experiences had shaped their existence. All in all, I was trying their patience, which did not facilitate subsequent interviews, and eventually I was forced to seek additional sources such as books about Chinese immigration.

I did, however, learn some new things about the woman who almost despised talking about herself or self-boasting as she thought it to be. If one had to inform others of one's accomplishments, then they must not have been very worthwhile or others would have recognized them on their own—that was her attitude. Confidence was one thing, which, incidentally, she had plenty of, but false pride was a trait she and my grandfather would not tolerate, and often they verbally shot down those who were unjustifiably too lofty. (I feel this is an ideal time to begin her story so that others may be able to get acquainted with this woman.)

Miss Gee Ying was born July 18, 1904, in feudal Canton, China. She was raised in a small village by her mother and her uncle who lived nearby, since her father had died before she was 5 years old. Most of my relatives described her childhood as "typical," whatever that may mean since no one could give any specific examples of typical childhood activities in China. More often than not, all they offered as an answer were "rural," "agricultural," "farmer," "peasant," etc. Strangely enough, my mother does not recall her mother ever "picking up a plow, let alone plowing and harvesting." She did not have much schooling as most girls were not permitted to earn high levels of education at that time. In 1923, when she was 19, the village matchmaker arranged a marriage between her and Quong Chin, an educated young man of 19 from a nearby village. Although they had never met before, he seemed a good match since he and his four brothers were among the few who had a high level of education. A year later, on July 28, she gave birth to a daughter, Tam Lan Fong. When the daughter was 2 years old, Quong Chin decided to leave for America to seek a better life for his family. He had to go alone because the Immigration Act of 1924, passed by Congress, specifically excluded 'Chinese women, wives, and prostitutes.' He was headed for the Gold Mountain (aptly named by the Chinese after the Gold Rush of the 1800s) but could only obtain traveling papers for Mexico. From there he stowed away on board a ship headed for San Francisco. My mother recalls his speaking of a large metal bowl which he used at times of frequent seasickness. No doubt, it must have been a long and agonizing journey, not to mention illegal. When he arrived, he discovered that even those who entered the country legally had a very slim chance of gaining citizenship because of the provisions of the Immigration Act, which distinguished foreign travelers into two categories: 'Immigrants' were admitted as permanent residents with the opportunity to become citizens eventually; the rest were admitted on a temporary basis and were not eligible for citizenship. The number of persons allowed in the category was set by law at one-sixth of one percent of the total population of that ancestry in the United States as of the 1920 census. The 1920 census had the lowest count of ethnic Chinese in this country since 1860. As a result, only 105 Chinese immigrants were permitted each year. Consequently, upon arriving in Louisiana, Quong Chin purchased a birth certificate, which stated that he was born in New Orleans to a Chinese man and an English woman, to ensure his citizenship. He was now known as Frank Thomas Chin.

He found several odd jobs—coal mining for a very brief time—but finally settled down with the mundane but safe profession of a waiter. From that he was to build his fortune to pay for his family's passage to America. He returned fourteen years later to Hong Kong where Gee Ying met him. There they conceived their second child. A daughter, Tam Nga Fong, was born July 14, 1941. Frank Thomas left soon after his visit. Because of his precarious citizenship status in America, he did not want to stay away too long lest he be discovered and denied reentrance. Again, he headed back alone since the Chinese immigrant quota was still the same 105. Although the U.S. Chinese Exclusion Act of 1882 (which banned the entrance of all Chinese laborers for ten years initially, but was extended indefinitely) was repealed that same year, "the Immigration and Naturalization Service claimed to be unable to find even (105) qualified Chinese. A 'Chinese' was defined as anyone with more than 50 percent Chinese blood, regardless of citizenship or country of residence."

However, in 1946, a separate law, exclusive of the War Bride Act, permitted wives and children of Chinese Americans to apply for entry as 'non-quota immigrants.' At this time, Frank Thomas anxiously filed the appropriate papers to have his wife sent over. In order to be granted his request to sponsor a woman from China, he needed to provide the immigration officials with a justifiable reason for doing so. He told the officials that during his last visit to Hong Kong in 1940, he got married to an 18-year-old woman who was visiting from Canton and she gave birth to their son a year later. It must be noted that this was a common practice among the Chinese, and possibly other immigrant groups. Many Chinese "legal citizens of the United States of America...had declared the birth of a new son for every year they had been visiting in China and thereby made 'slots for many paper sons.'" Furthermore, Frank Thomas adhered to the old Chinese notion that daughters are worthless beings: they cannot contribute much to the family in terms of physical labor or financial assistance and yet the family had to raise a dowry for them when they left the house to marry into another family; thus, the profit did not equal the large investment. At least, this is my mother's explanation for this gesture. She thinks her father believed a boy would have fared better and gained more from such an experience than would a girl—or two in this case. I only wish I could hear my grandmother's opinion. I am sure she had strong feelings about the entire situation but was not in a position at the time to air them.

Frank Thomas, though, did not have a son, but since adoptions among the Chinese have always been reluctantly considered, "the best choice for adoption is the son of a brother, not of a stranger." Luckily for him, he had a nephew who was just a few months younger than Tam Nga Fong. This "paper son" later became my Uncle John. Three years later, Gee Ying and her new "son" were on board an Air India airplane for a six-day journey to New York. They arrived here one December evening after the offices at Ellis Island were closed for the day and were forced to stay overnight for questioning the next morning. My uncle, John

Chin, who was 8 years old at the time, does not remember much of the place except that it was extremely crowded but clean. "There were people huddled in small crowds in the corners...because they were frightened of the new environment.... I was scared too and tired; it was a long trip. The plane stopped in the Philippines, England, and somewhere else. Your grandmother was scared too, but she tried to hide it from me so that I wouldn't cry. She kept telling me that the place we were going to was going to be very different. We would start a new life there and would make more money there." John Chin was not the most helpful source since he has bitter feelings about being adopted and taken far from his parents, none of which he wanted to address.

They were released the next day because they had the proper traveling papers. My grandfather met them and brought them to their apartment on East 13th Street in Manhattan. My uncle remembers the apartment as do I, for they lived there for over twenty years. Although the neighborhood progressively worsened, they never felt the desire to move. They knew everyone in the building and were very content with their surroundings. No amount of urging by my parents and other family members would budge them. They finally settled into another apartment near City Hall to be closer to the senior citizen center, which they daily frequented. They used to walk to Chinatown from their apartment, regardless of the weather. My grandfather used to carry home a twenty-five pound bag of rice because he thought the rice in Chinatown was better than the store brands in the supermarket.

Five years later, my grandmother encountered Mew. It was a striped male tabby who took an instant liking to her. She took it in despite my grandfather's objections. According to him, cats were not to be trusted, but she welcomed it into the house nevertheless. My uncle claims the cat was diseased and that is why he tried to get rid of it. It seems very difficult to believe either of them in contrast to the way my grandmother described it: friendly, obedient and loyal, as far as cats go. When she returned from the hospital after her gall bladder operation and appendectomy, Mew used to snuggle up next to her to provide warmth for her healing sutures and to offer a bit of comfort. Such rapport between cat and master is rare, but she managed to achieve it. Her actions toward the cat reveal many things about her. Her decision to keep the cat despite my grandfather's and uncle's objections is one example of how she stood up for her beliefs. She was not the typical demure and submissive Chinese wife. I suppose growing up with a part-time father (her uncle) and one older brother did not train her well to become a subservient woman. She had to depend on herself for the most part. Both she and her mother lived without many male figures. Perhaps the lack of male control or influence strengthened them. Her father died when she was 2 and her mother carried on alone. She never remarried for various reasons. And when Gee Ying was married, her husband left for America and was gone for twenty-three years before she was reunited with him. Furthermore, my mother and aunt recall how authoritarian my grandfather used to be, but somehow he never had full reign over his wife. The coupling of these two strong people made for frequent and heated arguments, but in the end they balanced each other out. Their steadfast attitudes kept one another in check.

Her nurturing and mothering-with-a-distance is truly exemplified with the cat. My grandmother was never very affectionate. She rarely hugged or kissed anyone, but if anyone counted on other expressions of love and kindness, one would surely not be disappointed and would find she had an ample supply of them. She told me cats were too

independent to be named. My guess is that she feared at-
tachments. The first half of her life involved being separated
from those she loved, whether by death or physical distance.
In all cases, love was synonymous with pain and separation.
In this sense, one can see why she avoided smothering-type
relationships. Her fear of attachment and her independent
nature did not allow her to expect anyone to stay around for
long periods of time. The cat, I think, represented the perfect
outlet for her to pour out her emotions safely. She never
expected the cat to reciprocate her feelings and yet Mew
desperately needed the affection. The guilt she felt as a result
of leaving her family, especially her 9-year-old daughter, was
also manifested in her relationship with the cat. She gave it
extra attention to compensate for her inability to provide any
to her daughters. Furthermore, toilet-training a cat is un-
doubtedly a difficult task and the fact that she accomplished
it is an indication that she possessed a good deal of patience
and understanding. Taking the time to purchase fresh liver
for Mew is a small-scale example of her generosity. When I
asked my mother what others thought of her, she used a
Chinese phrase, "big-mouthed one," which literally means
her pockets and bags were all wide open so that the contents
would be easily accessible to all.

About a year later, Mew was gone off to wander else-
where. My grandmother always talked of his departure as
an inevitable fact, never with any sorrow or regret. That
year, my grandparents decided to send over their second
daughter. To do that, another story had to be devised for the
immigration officials. This time they claimed Tam Nga Fong
was Gee Ying's daughter from a previous marriage (to Mr.
Tam.) He had joined the military and had been gone since
1939 and was presumed dead in 1941; the war in China was
in full scale by then. To solidify their story, they made her a

year older, on paper, so that all the events coincided with their claims.

In December 1958, Tam Nga Fang arrived by plane at Kennedy International. Her parents met her and for the first time she met her father. She had only heard stories of him until then. Her mother looked vaguely the same, but her outward appearance was different. The true extent of Gee Ying's transformation would not be immediately evident to my mother. For the moment, she seemed to be the same person she knew nine years before.

Indeed, Gee Ying had changed quite a bit since arriving at the shores of America. Looking at pictures of her in China is like looking at the rural counterpart of the urban Gee Ying. The first time I got a glimpse of the old, pre-America Gee Ying was after her death. Not only were the clothes and hair different, her countenance did not seem familiar. She never smiled in any of the pictures—as if she knew what her fate would be. She never mentioned these pictures to anyone, not to be secretive about them but rather because she did not think they were of any significance. The past was gone forever.

When she first arrived, Frank Thomas had already been here over twenty years and therefore was willing and able to teach her everything she needed to know. Acting much like the pioneering social workers in America who sought to make the assimilation process a smooth transition for the immigrants, he was sympathetic to her situation, yet determined to see her adapt to the new customs. She must have wanted to do so herself, for she was not the type of person who sacrificed her principles in order to yield to another's wishes. This held true her entire life. Her first job here is a case in point. She started in a clothes factory in Chinatown, but she soon found the conditions unbearable and, consequently, quit. Although they needed the extra money to support John, she refused to return to a job that demeaned her. She adamantly maintained her position when her relatives, including her sister in- law, tried to persuade her to reconsider. She did find a second job, making jewelry, in which she was forced to learn English since she was the only Chinese-speaking person there and her co-workers were either Italian, Jewish or Hispanic.

By the time my mother arrived from Hong Kong, Gee Ying had begun taking extra work home for additional income because they were also expecting the arrival of their newly adopted son, Thomas Chin, the following year. My mother and grandmother alike adopted most of the American customs upon their arrivals. They did, however, retain the language and continued to prepare Chinese food for their respective families. My grandfather took John and Gee Ying shopping their first week here so that at least they would look like New Yorkers. Once clad in Western garb, she was prepared for more and her avid love of shopping sprung to life. From that time on, she used any excuse to shop for clothes. It must be noted that she was not a frivolous shopper flitting around and buying everything in sight. She carefully inspected all her purchases and looked for the best bargains. She loved shopping in the Delancey area, for the close proximity of the shops offered the largest selection in the smallest amount of space. The next best place was a large department store.

Every week, Gee Ying went to the movies either with my mother or her female friends. She loved the cinema and the Palladium was a very short walk away. There were also theatres in Chinatown which offered movies in Mandarin with English and Chinese subtitles. She once told me that when she first arrived, both the American and Chinese movies were alien to her because only the very educated spoke Mandarin. She finally settled on those in English for their usefulness and their variety. When she did not go to the movies, she went to the park on 15th Street and Second Avenue to feed the pigeons. I used to think that she took me to the park for my enjoyment because, after a while, I would ask to go, but in effect she instilled the pleasure in me.

I have always considered her my surrogate mother because I was already spending weekends with her by the time I was 3 or 4 months old. Grandparents, to me, were those whom children saw only during holidays and special occasions. I spent so much time with them that unless gifts or large elaborate meals were present, I could not distinguish between ordinary days and holidays with them.

Of all their grandchildren, my brother and I spent the most time with them. This was largely due to the fact that my cousins spent their childhood in Hong Kong and when they arrived, they had already reached puberty. Yet, even my cousin, Richard Lee, my youngest cousin, who is 3 years my senior, did not spend much time with them except during the holidays. It was my grandfather's idea to take us to the Thanksgiving parade every year. My brother and I would sleep over the night before so that we would get an early start in the morning to claim a good spot with the best vantage point. My grandmother would always buy us hot chocolate and my grandfather, peanuts. When we returned to my house for dinner, my grandmother always had a solid chocolate turkey in her pocketbook for each of us. Oddly enough, they were never crushed or misshaped by the crowd at the parade. Christmas always meant, to me, solid chocolate Santas.

Her consistency was evident in other respects as well. My mother recalls the old Italian woman who lived next door to my grandparents. She was a petite woman of 80 when my mother met her. For years, the woman and my grandmother traded things year round. Whenever the old woman made rum cookies, she brought some over for my grandmother, who would reciprocate in kind whenever she baked. Every Christmas, they would trade little gifts, nothing extravagant, for the woman lived off her social security checks. One day when the water boiler broke down in the middle of winter, my grandmother boiled pots of water and brought them over to the woman's apartment so that she could take her medicated bath.

Although my grandmother worked at her job at 36th Street and Fifth Avenue making jewelry for nearly forty years, she was not eligible for social security when she retired at age 75 because she entered the country as an 18-year-old woman, when, in actuality, she was 36. Therefore at 75 she was officially only 57.

Of all my sources, my mother has been the main link to the past. She was quite helpful with all the facts, although they were a bit limited. While she has assimilated the American lifestyle, she still has a strong attachment to her homeland. Within my family, there is virtually no one interested in visiting that part of the world from which our forebears came. Most of us have been taught that the past is gone forever. My parents have toured the Orient, but they never set foot inside mainland China. What puzzles me is that no one has any curiosity about our past. Those who lived through it have forgotten it and those who did not are not that interested in it. Now that my curiosity has been raised, I cannot find enough people who are willing to devote the time for idle conversations about our history. Perhaps if I show them this paper, I might be able to raise their curiosity as well.

Bibliography:

Hsu, Francis L. K. *The Challenge of the American Dream: The Chinese in the United States.* (Belmont, California: Wadworth Publishing, 1971).

Kingston, Maxine Hong, *China Man* (New York: Alfred A. Knopf, 1977).

My special thanks to my mother, Helen Yee, nee Tam Nga Fong; my uncle, John Y. Chin and my aunt, Mrs. Ching Yip Lee, nee Tam Lan Fong.

ilana alperstein

a s I sat at the kitchen table, I looked into my grandmother's eyes as she told me of the courage of my grandfather.

On December 7, 1941, the Japanese attacked Pearl Harbor and the United States declared war. Franklin D. Roosevelt was President and my grandfather, Martin Schlesinger, was a lawyer in Manhattan. He was a bachelor and a patriot, and somehow bored with his legal practice. He decided to join the army despite the fact that he didn't have to serve.

My grandfather joined as a private (the lowest rank) and was sent to Chicago to Officers' Candidate School, where he received intensive training and instruction in the Japanese language.

He sailed to the Philippine Islands, and later on to Korea. While on one of the Philippine islands, my grandfather was driving a car to pick up someone. Suddenly the man sitting right next to him was shot and killed. My grandfather escaped unharmed.

In Korea, my grandfather was appointed a military judge. Here are two cases he remembered. One case was about a woman charged with murder. It turned out that her husband left her for another woman. She was angry. She invited the other woman for a talk at the top of a hill. The angry wife then pulled the woman down the hill by the hair. When they reached the bottom, the rival was dead. My grandpa set the wife free, saying, "What is to be accomplished by keeping her in jail?"

The second case was about a man who was in jail for being a communist. "What did he do?" asked my grandpa. "He's a communist" was the answer. "But what did he do?" asked my grandpa again. As an American lawyer, he knew you couldn't be charged for what you think, but only for what you do. He set the man free. In gratitude, the man's wife and daughter stayed up all night and embroidered three beautiful flowers on rice silk. The flowers stand for love, hope and life. They are now framed in my grandparents' house. When I grow up, I will tell these stories to my children.

I have many documents from my grandpa's military service. I have a letter of commendation, a picture on a scroll, medals, stripes and stars that he received.

My grandpa used to say that the years he served in the army were his shining years, even though he could have been rich if he had practiced law during the war. The other proud moment was marrying my grandma, but that is another story.

This story makes me very proud. It make me love my grandpa even more to hear how much he loved his country and how he had the courage to act upon his love. It also tells me a very important thing about the legal system, which allows freedom of thought. I am deeply touched by the picture of the flowers as a token of gratitude.

Ilana Alperstein, Yaffa Schlesinger's granddaughter, is a student in SUNY Albany. This essay was written when she was in Russell Sage High School in Forest Hills, New York. It won first prize in a competition *Stories my Grandparent Told Me* sponsored by the Police Athletic League and McGraw-Hill (December 21, 1990). Her grandfather, Martin Schlesinger, would be pleased to see his story in this book.

steven zhou

I was feeling under the weather on September 27. If you would check your records, they would show that I was absent on that day. I was home alone, recuperating from a cold. My grandmother, who lives in the same apartment building as I, came down to check on me. Obviously, news travels fast to a grandmother or perhaps it's her innate "grandmother instinct" that knows when a grandson is not feeling well. My grandmother and I sat down comfortably on the sofa and talked for two hours. As one conversation led to another, she started talking about herself. I was about to start my "grandmother interview paper" and I didn't even know it at the time. I was happily drawn into her stories. She did most of the talking and I did most of the listening. The information I received couldn't have been drawn out by a mere "interview" because I wouldn't know what specific questions to ask or if there were such questions. As I listened to her, all I could ask was "when, why and how." I wanted her stories in great depth. The information was not only for the purpose of this paper but also for myself. It is a part of my family history.

In this paper, I will try my best to translate her every word into English. I am sure that no matter how hard I try, some of the essence of her stories will be lost because some of it simply cannot be put into words. Here I present to you my grandmother, Suk Ying Yan.

> I am now 67 years old. I have seen much horror in my days. I have suffered as much as anyone. I watched my father die when I was only 17 years old, you know. See, my village was based on the side of the Communist Party, and Taiwan's Nationalist Party bordered my village. There was great political and power tension. My village and its people were the victims. Our government didn't give a damn for my village and its people. The good men in my village were always taken away, beaten and tortured by the Taiwanese army. Beaten just for those bastards' entertainment.

> I've seen with my own eyes respectable men getting every joint in their fingers burned by cigarettes. Some even got their bodies burned black. The soldiers with a metal foil that was burned red would wrap it around their bodies. I can still hear the sizzling sound and smell of human flesh burning. There were men with their heads cracked wide open by the soldiers, using a brick. Their bodies were thrown away like trash. Some families risked their lives to try to "steal" the bodies back for proper burial.

> Well, they took my father because they accused him of stealing their weapons, which he never did. They kicked, punched and simply beat him senseless for nothing, just for their entertainment. When they let my father go, my brother had already gone into hiding and I was just married to your grandfather. Your grandfather

reluctantly agreed to let me go see my father. My father was dying. I didn't know what to do, so I told my father that I would go get brother. My father grabbed me by the arm and kept repeating the words "êm põ" (which means "don't"). He said that he was going to die anyway and he didn't want brother to die also. With a low dragging "êm põ," he died. He was only 39 years old. [My grandmother's voice was trembling and with tears in her eyes, she continues]. To this day, when reading the newspaper, I never read the Taiwan section of it. I just couldn't. And when I see people being tortured, even in the movies, I just cover my eyes like this [she demonstrates by lowering her head with her two hands firmly placed over her eyes]. It's just too painful.

I had your father when I was 19 years old. That was the time I knew that I must find a way out of all the madness. For the next fourteen years, I surveyed my surroundings, which were like an untamed jungle. A friend, myself, and a few other people were searching for the best pathway to the Hong Kong border. We did our searching in the night and hid in the day. We must have fed thousands of leeches in our endless search. [A smile finally appears on her face.]

Finally, we decided on a pathway. It was a stream that was about three feet deep. It was an extremely bushy area, One could only see things that were about ten feet from where one stood. At the end of that path was a fence that separated China from Hong Kong. Back at home, we took a few days to plan our final move and gather the things we needed. My mother told me to leave my father behind because what we were going to do was very dangerous. I reluctantly agreed to do so. However, my friend had decided to bring her daughter along. So in the year '62 we made our move.

We crawled along the stream with only our heads above water. We took it an inch at a time. We would, as before, do our traveling at night and hiding in the day. We hid in anything that offered cover—bushes, trees, rocks, small caves, just about anything. Many of us got sick. My friend's daughter became extremely sick. Her sickness quickly led to her death. My friend and I barely had time to dig her a grave. To this day, my friend still blames herself for the death of her daughter. Along the way we ate anything that was eatable—leaves, fruits, insects and everything else. A couple of months later we were at the fence.

The fence was about twenty to thirty feet tall. The top was sharply hooked toward us. On the darkest night, we climbed the fence rapidly and nervously. I made it over safely. However, my friend was not so lucky. She must have forgotten about the hooked top in her nervousness. She had severely pierced her head and was losing much blood. We were both panicky. I remembered that when my mother had stepped on a long nail, she would stop the flow of blood by placing fresh chewed grass on her wound, so that was what I did. I pulled a handful of grass, put it in my mouth, chewed it and placed it on my friend's wound. It really did stop the bleeding. We were both so relieved.

We were on Hong Kong soil now and we had to find places to hide again. There were always Hong Kong border guards checking the ground. We had stupidly hid ourselves in an abandoned hut that was used as a restroom. We were found almost immediately by a guard. We were so scared. We got on our knees and begged the guard to let us go. The guard finally took pity on us. He told us to go away quickly and he'd pretend he hadn't seen anything. My friend and I disappeared faster than a ghost [another smile]. We went to our planned destination and waited for my friend's uncle for a day.

The uncle showed up with a truck carrying many large barrels. He told us to hide quietly inside two empty barrels. Even though it was a really rough ride, I was as quiet as a mouse. I did not dare to move. After about an hour, we finally made it to the uncle's apartment. I lived there for a couple of months because I had very little money.

I was able to make some money because of my sewing skills. I tried to save every penny that I made. I worked hard in Hong Kong for eight years. I made enough money to invest in new buildings for two years. I was more financially secure than most people in Hong Kong then, even the natives.

One day my friend told me that she was going to immigrate to the United States because she had relatives there. I told her to find a way to bring me over as well. I would pay her back any legal fees. She asked me why I would want to go the United States since I was doing so well in Hong

Kong. She warned me that I would probably have to start over in the United States. I told her that all the money I had was meaningless if I didn't have my family. I can't take the money with me to the grave. If I was to die alone, in Hong Kong, life would be so empty. I wanted to bring your father's family over. My friend saw my reasoning and agreed to do so.

I immigrated to the United States in 1973 and settled there rather quickly. I used what money I had to buy this apartment building. Buildings were cheaper then. I had to continue to work in garment factories in Chinatown to make as much money as I could. I sometimes would walk to Chinatown (from Queens) just to save the transportation fee. I went to school at night to earn my citizenship. Finally on February 28, 1982, I met my family once again.

After that sentence, my grandmother sighed and told me that she had to go up to her apartment to make a phone call. She told me to get some rest as she exited through the door. I did not stop her because I knew the rest of the story that took place on and after February 28, 1982. I was 6 years old then. I remember taking a cab for the first time in my life from Kennedy Airport to my new home. I had never seen so many lights before. Outside an apartment building, there was an elderly woman eagerly waiting for her son and daughter. Dropping the luggage, my father and aunt ran to the elderly woman and hugged her. They were all crying. I had never seen my father cry before. It was a strange feeling and I didn't understand it. As I think back, that was the most beautiful moment that I've ever witnessed in my life.

I think my grandmother had always wanted to tell me of her past, but I never gave her or myself an opportunity. I knew that my grandmother had to work hard all her life. I knew that she worked in many garment factories in Chinatown. I knew that she had worked twelve hours a day, seven days a week. Her sweat was on each dollar that she made. I always knew that she worked hard, but I never knew just how hard until now. It seems that she started to work the day that she was born. She's retired now. She deserves to live her golden years happily and freely as much as anyone in this world. It is a privilege to call such a strong woman my grandmother.

camela mazella

"Italia, my homeland," he began, "is rather small com
pared to the U.S.A., especially the part where I was
born—Ischia." This is the beginning, well, maybe the
middle, of the story of an incredible man I will try convey to
you here. *Il mio nonno* (my grandfather) is from a little island
in the Bay of Naples, or Napoli as he refers to it. There on
this island he was born and raised to be the best Italian man
he could be. Born in Mintorno in the hills of Ischia, he remembers many things about life there, but his most vivid
memories are of World War II in which he fought for his
paese (country) and was captured. At 76, *il mio nonno*
Alessandro Rasile is a very strong man who had to live
through many trials. This is one of those trials.

It all began on a cool morning when an officer knocked
at the door to the villa. "He was no more then a boy himself
and he asked to speak to me and my brother. I knew before
he spoke what was going on. I had heard that the President
had declared war on Germany and I knew it was my turn to
fight." Neither of the boys questioned their call, they
wouldn't dare. There was no such thing as a draft dodger
then. Honor played too important a role in the lives of all
Italians. "You would never dishonor your family nor your
paese. We knew we would be called. In Italia we must fight in

our military from the age of 18 if the government so chooses." That afternoon he and his brother were on their way to boot camp with only what could be carried on their backs and with big hugs and kisses from a mother who they wouldn't see again. But let's not get ahead of ourselves.

They arrived together at the camp but soon were separated to go on different paths. It was a rough two weeks of training. "Every morning we were up by dawn and had an hour of exercise. Then we'd eat bread with butter and drink coffee. After that we learned how to use the guns and tactics. This went on for two weeks. Then we were sent out to fight."

The battles were bloody and there were far too many casualties. Death was seen everywhere and food was short. "In one battle I remember going into the forest and being taken by surprise. My sergeant and I got down and just started shooting—there was no time to ask questions. All I kept thinking was that these were all boys, we were boys fighting in a man's world. Then I heard a scream." The scream he later would learn was his sergeant. He was shot. The wound was in the leg and it didn't seem fatal. The shot hadn't hit any major blood vessels. He dragged the sergeant's body further into the woods and took out his knife and proceeded to take the bullet out. He then tore his pants leg and tied it around the sergeant's body to stop the bleeding. Unfortunately, he wasn't paying attention to his surroundings.

His concentration on his friend and sergeant left him oblivious to the soldiers who soon surrounded them. They were both captured by German soldiers. "They were going to shoot Giovanni (the sergeant), but I pleaded with them to let me carry him. They told me to get up and I was sure that they would kill me, but they didn't. They told me to walk, and one of the soldiers picked up Giovanni and carried him.

It felt like we walked miles when we finally stopped. Then I realized we did. We crossed the border and I found I was on my way toward Russia. That first night all I did was look after the sergeant. I thought if I slept they would shoot him."

Il mio nonno had many memories of being held captive with Giovanni, but many were very painful and I did not want to push him. He was in many situations where he was almost killed. Once he found himself on a line of people who were all being shot and then fell forward into a mass grave, but he was pulled off at the end to carry a soldier's equipment because the soldier was wounded. By this time Giovanni was walking on his own and helped him carry the soldier's stuff, so he was also spared. His memories are extremely painful and just show how cruel these people were and how evil human nature can be. The most disturbing one he told me involved a child, a baby girl. I'll let him tell it in his own words.

"It was a sunny day *sensa* [without a] cloud in the sky. We'd been walking through the night and we finally stopped in a village. It seemed to be deserted but soon we found out it wasn't. One family remained behind and made the mistake of believing that we were the Allies coming to help. There were twenty of us at this point. Five of us were prisoners and the rest soldiers. A man came out of a small villa and he wasn't allowed to even say a word before they opened fire. You can't imagine how a body looks after being shot at such a close range. I prayed he was the only one, but he wasn't; a woman ran from the back of the house. The commander ran after her and caught her. In her arms was a child of 3. She was beautiful with big blue eyes and long black hair like her mom. He dragged this woman till she was in front of all his men and then he undressed her. They each took a turn raping her in front of her daughter. If that wasn't bad enough they went to touch the little girl. An officer thought it would be nice to have a little fresh *'puta'*—in English it is equivalent to the female body part. The mother tried to grab her child and they shot her—a direct chest wound. The child screamed. One soldier grabbed her and held her. He told her not to be like her mommy but she was just a child. They made us get up and walk away but I turned around. The soldiers were all walking but one remained. He put the little girl by her mother, in her arms, and shot her. She didn't even cry."

Tears came down my grandfather's cheek as well as mine. I can't imagine what it was like. Thank God soon they were traded to the Russians who set them free. They all began a trek back to Italia. They walked for days and soon months. They didn't even know the war was over until they finally reached Italy and the people helped them, recognizing their uniforms, and told them it was over. He had heard nothing about his family for three years. All they were told was that he had been captured. Nobody thought he'd return; most didn't.

He was to face another trial now; the pain didn't end when the war did. You see, when the war was over, his mom, dad and youngest sister returned to their home. This was a month before the return of my grandfather. They went into the house and didn't know the house had been used for the storage of gun powder. His mom went to light the stove so she could cook and the house exploded. There was no way out and the flames were horrible, at least that is what he was told. They never knew he was okay.

He returned to Napoli to get the ferry to go home and he found his sister returning with his brother, the brother who had been in the war with him. He had been shot in the leg and returned home wounded. He had only fought a year. His sister told him what had happened and all he remembers is that he didn't get to say goodbye and let them know he was safe. After all he had gone through—two years as a prisoner—he still was being bombarded by the pains of war. Life did eventually get better.

He still keeps in touch with his friend Giovanni, and he says that he doesn't regret fighting for his country but does regret not standing up for the others who died in front of him. In wartime, decisions are made quickly and the sadistic side of human nature comes out as well as the intense terror of it all. Now at 76 this just seems to be a distant part of his life. One chapter in a book of many.

yelena yukhananova

We were sitting in the kitchen and having dinner when I asked my grandmother to tell me something about her childhood. She sat deeply in the chair and, looking in the space between us, began her story.

My dear, my childhood was not easy. As you probably know, I was born in 1927 in a small town in Russia. You'll be surprised, however, to learn that your great-grandparents adopted me on the tenth day of my life. I found out about this much, much later in my life, but I never had any regrets about it. My parents were a wonderful Jewish couple. Their first child died, and my mom was told by a doctor that she would never be able to have kids again. My parents decided to take the child into their family and raise that child as their own.

During that period, between the October Revolution and World War II, Jews in Russia were being severely persecuted and discriminated against. My parents had to change their last name from Millerman to Rishkov. My parents tried to speak less and less Yiddish at home. We quietly spent holidays such as Rosh Hashanah and Passover at home. Russian people were greatly prejudiced against Jews and were blaming them for all the bad things happening to the people. My parents were afraid for their safety. They were afraid that if they would continue with all their Jewish traditions, I would certainly become an orphan. My mother couldn't let it happen, so she joined the Communist Party. This decision solved all our problems. My parents were very happy to see that nobody in my high school could tell me that I was Jewish and that there was no place there for people like me, because in all my documents, in the paragraph under "Nationality," "Russian" was written. I was happy to be accepted into Pioneers and later to become a leader of Komsomol in high school. Our family became more and more like Russians in every way. We started to celebrate Christmas and New Year like everyone else. My parents weren't against it because they knew that deep down they were still Jewish. One thing they still did was to light candles on Jewish holidays and quietly read the prayers. I loved my parents for it—they were smart and strong people.

July 22, 1941. I remember that day as the worst day of my life. All plans that I had about the future, about going to a prestigious university and later finding a job, were destroyed. My father was drafted. We were left all alone. I was 15 when I got my first job working in a war factory. I had to work because everything that we had we would send to my father who was fighting on the front lines. Everything such as money, food, clothes, cigarettes. In our town, as in many others, there was starvation. A lot of people died because there was nothing to eat. Diseases such as murrain and typhus carried away many people's lives.

My father sent us letters once a month. In every letter he told my mother to take good care of me. He also thanked us for the warm sweaters and socks that my mother handknitted herself. Each time he told us that the war was coming to an end and that he'd see us soon. Each time when we read his letter we cried and with each letter our hopes grew that soon we'd see him alive and well.

It was in December 1944 when my mother and I received a letter from the Soviet army that F. Rizhkov had died in battle defending his country. My mother cried for a whole week. She couldn't eat or drink anything. But still she had to go to work every day or else she would risk being thrown into prison. This was wartime—tough period and tough policies came with it.

May 9, 1945. End of war. That day was one of the happiest in my life. We couldn't believe it. My mother cried and laughed at the same time. She was happy for other women whose husbands returned home.

My mother and I decided to move out of our town to Middle Asia, where my mother's cousin and his family lived. Mother's relatives helped us to build a small house where we then lived for thirty years. I graduated from high school when I was 20 years old. Then I graduated from university and became a history teacher.

My grandmother stopped and looked at her clock. Without her saying it I knew it was time for me to go to bed.

kit wai chan

I was born into a big family in China. I have four brothers and I am the fourth-oldest. Until the time I was 6 years old I lived with all of my brothers. At that time my parents, two of my brothers and I moved out of the village to Macao. Two of my oldest brothers stayed in the village because they were over 16 years of age at the time. My grandparents died a long time ago. Therefore, I can only interview my mother to write a paper.

Although I have four brothers, we have rarely lived together and we now live in different cities. My parents have a very oldfashioned way of thinking. They don't like life in the village. They think that if people move far from the village, they will have a better future. Therefore, they always want to leave the village. At home, I always had different ideas from them. So there are some conflicts between me and them. In the interview I will ask my mother some questions about her life.

I have had three immigration experiences. In 1979, when I was 6 years old, my mother brought my third-oldest brother, my younger brother and me to Macao. Macao is a Portuguese colony and it has a different policy from the Chinese government. When I was there, I also received some different culture and education. My partial family stayed for eight years. And then we moved to Hong Kong to live with my father. Six years later, my parents, my younger brother and I came to America. However, my third-oldest brother could not come with us because he was over 21 at that time. So my family members have always lived in different places. I know that it was not easy for them to move their home so many times. I want to know more about what feelings they have now. Therefore, I made an interview with my mother today.

This morning we went to Chinatown to eat dim-sum for our breakfast. After breakfast, we went to market to buy the food for the following week. When my mother sat in front of the table to prepare the dinner, I started to talk to her.

"Mom, do you remember when you married, and how old you were at the time?" I asked.

She said, "I married your father in 1961. I was 21."

"How did you know father?"

"It is a long story. At that time, ladies did not make friends directly. Moreover, we had no rights to decide our marriage. Our parents chose the men to be our husbands. Your father was introduced to me by a matchmaker."

"So, you mean my grandparents made the decision to marry for you?" I asked.

"Almost."

"Had you met father before?"

"Yes," she said. "It was so wonderful that I had met your father three times outside the village before we knew each other. I remember that he was on a bicycle. He had just come back to the village from Hong Kong."

"Really!" I replied. "After thirty-six years, how do you feel about your marriage?"

"It is OK. Good!" She was smiling.

My mother is very Chinese traditional in her thinking. She rarely talks about her love story openly. Therefore, when I asked her so many questions about this, she was embarrassed. She also felt uncomfortable. Although she said that her marriage was "OK," she enjoys it very much. I do not recall ever seeing them argue with each other. During most of their thirty-six years of marriage, they have not lived together. My father always worked in Hong Kong. He came back to the village only a few times a year. My mother always wished to go to Hong Kong to live with him.

I continue to ask my mother questions.

"Mom, what made you want to go to Hong Kong?"

"I wanted to live with your father," she replied. "However, I waited for twenty-six years to get to Hong Kong because many people were waiting for that."

"But we still could not move to Hong Kong directly," I said.

In 1979, as I mentioned earlier, my mother brought my third-oldest brother, my younger brother and me to Macao, not Hong Kong. She said that she was anxious about whether we could rent an apartment. Moreover, she missed two of my older brothers who remained in the village. Later my mother felt better. I finished elementary school there. I made many friends, too. After eight years in Macao, we finally got the permit and we moved to Hong Kong. We started a new life there.

"You were very happy at that time, right?" I asked her.

"At the beginning, I had many conflicts in my mind. I was happy, but I was worried because the standard of living in Hong Kong was very high. Everything was very expensive. Fortunately, I found a job as an office cleaner."

"Mom, how did you feel about the job?" I asked.

"It was the first job in my life and it was the first time I made money myself. At that period, I was very happy," she replied.

"So, why did you make the decision to immigrate to the U.S.? Did you have fears about Hong Kong's return to China in 1997?"

"In the U.S., you and your brother can go to the universities easier than in Hong Kong. And we can have a better future here," she said.

In fact, I think she feared the Chinese government and its policies. In 1967, the "cultural revolution" began, and many Chinese had had hard times in that era. They could not forget their experiences. My mother told me about her own experience. During this time, students farmed. They spent half of their school time farming and the other half studying. If students did not work on a farm, they did not have any food. People disliked this system. As a result, my mother gave up school in the eighth grade. And then she married my father.

During the '70s, the government carried out a new birth control law. Each family could have only one child. If people defied this law, they had to pay a strict penalty. When my mother became pregnant during this time, the officer tried to force her to abort the baby. My mother refused to do this. Finally, she had my younger brother. As a result, my family was severely penalized. We could not have food distributed to us. Food distribution was then controlled by the government. People could not buy food in the market, even if they had money. Therefore, my father sent food to us from Hong Kong and was afraid to come back to the village for several years. All of these things made my mother fear communism. I think that is one of the reasons my mother decided to emigrate to America.

However, my mother does not like life in America because she and my father don't speak English. They are afraid to go out without our guidance. They have no special hobby in New York. I think that cooking is the most important and interesting work for them every weekend.

"Will you go back to Hong Kong?" I asked her.

"Maybe, maybe not! I am not sure yet. I can't give you an answer." she replied.

"In your life, what events are unforgettable?"

"The fire that happened at home in the village. We nearly lost our home. Fortunately, our neighbor discovered it and put it out early. This was a terrible memory."

I had heard this story many times before. It happened on a summer night. Electricity was not that common at the time. My elder brother was using a candle to study in his room. When he left his room to take a break, the candle was over turned by the wind. His paper caught fire. As a result, his room was burned before the fire was put out. My mother watched the fire and was nearly overwhelmed at the time.

At the end, I asked my mother, "What is most important in your life?"

"Health," she answered very quickly and added, "I hope everybody has good health."

In her traditional Chinese thinking, my mother believes our ancestors give luck to us. Therefore, during every Chinese festival she worships the ancestors and also asks them for what our family needs. She always hopes that my older brothers can get immigration visas, so we can live together in the U.S.

tifara markovits

my grandmother's name is Tzortil Samuel Markovits. She was born in Velky Polad, Czechoslovakia, on April 1, 1923. My grandmother was raised as an Orthodox Jew. She lived on a farm with three brothers and a sister. Every morning she would get up early to milk the cows, make cheese and wash the laundry by hand. My grandmother said that she would be up with the rooster so that when the men came home from the synagogue, at six in the morning, she and her mother would have fresh bread, yeast cakes and pastries ready for them to eat and take out to the fields. Life wasn't easy and they had a lot of work to do. She had a saying in Yiddish, *"no poidony, no matzaloni,"* which means that no one can get out of work. My great-grandmother was a "finster," meaning she helped all the women in the community pray because she was the only one who knew how to read. She was also a seamstress and taught the local girls how to sew.

My grandmother went to school until the eighth grade. After the Hungarians came in 1939, the Jews had to sit in the back of the classroom and weren't allowed to participate.

I asked my grandmother how she had fun. She answered, "We had fun, but different fun than you have here." She had friends whom she went to dancing school with and they would embroider together. There was one guy, named Weisslotsky, who liked my grandmother. He was very cute. Before the war they wanted to get married, but his parents didn't want them to. Weisslotsky's parents said that my grandmother was not good enough for their son. After the war he wanted to marry my grandmother, but she refused him. When he heard that my grandmother was engaged to be married, he offered her a cow to leave my grandfather. She didn't accept the offer.

The first time my grandmother met my grandfather, she said, "I could never marry him." My grandmother occasionally went to visit her brother, Amman, who lived in a neighboring town. During one visit Amman said, "there is someone I would like for you to meet. His name is Shmiel." My grandmother was 16 years old at the time, and she said, "I will not go out with him. He's 28 years old." I asked my grandmother how her parents reacted, and she said they trusted her and supported her decision. After the war Shmiel went to visit Amman and my grandmother was there. She recalled.

"[There was] no love between us, we were just friends. It was very strange because he came back after the war and we just started talking about marriage. One day he said he would call me [in those days the only phone was at the post office] and he didn't call. My friend said, 'He looks honest, he will call.' When he finally did call he apologized because he had just come out of prison."

My grandfather was a prominent man in Hungary after the war. The Hungarians thought that he was wealthy and they wanted his money, but he didn't have any so they threw him into jail. My grandparents got married because they didn't want to go out into the world alone. My grandmother said that she didn't love my grandfather before they got married but she grew to love him.

There was another man who wanted to marry my grandmother. He was a Jewish Czech soldier whom she met after
the war. He went home to see if anyone from his family
survived the war. When he went back to marry my grandmother, she was already engaged to marry my grandfather.

Amman and Moshe Wolf (another of my grandmother's
brothers) were taken to different labor camps when the
Hungarians came in 1938. Amman came back home after the
war, but Moshe Wolf never came back and no one knows
what happened to him. The third brother, Baila, was taken in
1940 to another labor camp, and after the war he met the
surviving family back home.

My great-grandfather was a very respected man in Velky
Polad. On the first night of Passover 1944, the Germans took
him because they thought he was a communist. The next
day the family learned that nine other prominent men in the
community had been taken as well. My grandmother and
her family tried to bribe the German officials to get my
great-grandfather back, but they took all the bribes without
giving a thing in return. He was never seen again.

Later that year my grandmother, great-grandmother, and
great-aunt Charlotte were taken to Auschwitz. Upon arrival
they were told to form a line and when they reached the
front of the line they were told to go to the right or to the
left. The left meant death, and right before my grandmother's eyes her mother was sent to the left. Those that
were sent to the right were told to undress completely. The
Germans cut off all of the hair from their bodies and took all
of their clothing and jewelry. This initiation to Auschwitz
robbed my grandmother of her pride, modesty and dignity,
which hurt more than the pilferage of their material things.
My grandmother and my great-aunt Charlotte were there for
six weeks. In July they were taken to Shtuthoff to work.
From Shtuthoff they were moved to different camps to work.

They were taken to Bumgarden and to Merzen. In January 1945 the Germans were running away from the Russians, who were defeating them. Once the Germans saw that their mission of destroying the entire non-Aryan race was not going to be completed, they wanted to destroy as many Jews as they could. So the Germans took 1,200 girls on a "death march." My grandmother and my great-aunt Charlotte were included. The Germans marched the girls in the snow and ice for miles and miles without any mercy. Whoever fell down or stumbled was shot in the head. Only 450 girls survived this "march." My grandmother marched the whole way with just a thin piece of cloth on her feet. In March 1945 the Russians finally freed them.

My grandmother said, "We were afraid of the Russians.... When the Russians were coming we were in tents made of wood. The Russians were bombing and we were so dumb we went out to look at the bombs and to see where they would land. We were so dumb."

The Russians took my grandmother, my great-aunt Charlotte and the other girls to work in a hospital called Danzig. I asked my grandmother how the Russians treated her and her friends. She said, "They [the Russians] weren't mean, but when they 'caught' a girl, she was finished. They would rape her and beat her. The Russians were drunks. We would try not to get too close to the Russians."

One night a Russian doctor called my grandmother, Gizzi and Shaindel to give a report. My grandmother was the head of caring for the sick, Gizzi was the head of the kitchen and Shaindel was the head of the lab. They went up to the quarters and saw a party, and my grandmother called out to her friends in Hungarian, "let's go!" Forty girls ran away from the hospital with only the clothes on their backs. They saw the Russians chasing after them, so they found their way back to Czechoslovakia. My grandmother and

Charlotte went home to Velky Polad. My great-uncle Baila was there and Amman came soon after. Together they went to the German DP camp to wait for a boat to go anywhere as long as it was out of Europe. Charlotte went to England on the children's transport and Amman went to Israel. My grandparents got married in the DP camp. "We found a Hungarian judge to marry us. And we went out in the world without anything—no money, no job, no nothing." Baila got married the next day to a girl who was in the camps with my grandmother.

On November 22, 1947, my grandparents, Baila and his wife finally boarded a boat to America. "We called the boat 'Mario Paigos,' because for seventeen days the ships couldn't dock because of high tides." My grandparents arrived in America with two suitcases of dirty diapers and an 11-month-old baby. They went to an organization called Hias. I asked my grandmother about government help and she said, "We didn't go on welfare because we were too proud to take anything from anyone. We were living in Brooklyn in a furnished room for seven and a half months. Then we moved in with an old man, because he paid eight dollars a week. I took care of him for three and a half years. Heshy was born in the apartment with the old man. A couple went in to take care of the old man after we left, for only six weeks. They said to me, 'How can you take it?' So I said, now I have some money."

My grandfather had trouble holding a job, because he wouldn't work on the Sabbath. Every Friday he said he was sick and gave excuses to his boss. But the boss would tell him that if he didn't come in on Saturday, he shouldn't come back in on Monday.

In 1953 they moved into an apartment on Amboy Street. After three and a half years of living with this old man they sent for Charlotte to come from England. My father was born on Amboy Street in 1953. At that time my grandfather got a job as a presser. My grandmother was at home with the kids and she had side jobs as a seamstress and making watch straps for a factory nearby. In 1955 my Aunt Evelyn was born. No one wanted kids in their apartment buildings so my grandparents bought a house on 104 Hopkinson Avenue. During the summer my grandparents got jobs as cooks in camps upstate. After the first summer as cooks they came home and bought a candy store, in 1959.

My grandmother always wanted to be a dietitian, but my grandfather didn't make enough money for her to go to school. In 1964 they bought a house on Linden Boulevard. From 1967 to 1974 my grandparents worked as cooks at Stern College. "We started there not knowing anything. Within two weeks I had the whole kitchen to myself." From 1974 to 1978 they worked as cooks at Long Beach Yeshiva. In 1975 my grandparents bought the house that my grand- mother has been living in now for twenty-two years.

From coming off the boat with two suitcases of dirty diapers, my grandparents have twenty-one grandchildren and one great-grandson. My grandparents call us their "interest," an apt description of what we are to them. They worked so hard and went through so much in their lives, and they considered that their investments had paid off. Their happiest moments now are watching their twenty-one grandchildren and one great-grandson grow up.

fumi ishikawa

ince my grandfather and the rest of my family live in
Japan, I had to depend on my mother to interview him
for me. Unfortunately, I was not able to contact him
directly, but my mother explained to me what he told her as
much as she could.

My grandfather, Shinji Moritani, was born on November
10, 1920, in the city called Shizuoka in Japan. He grew up
with many friendly people in a peaceful neighborhood.
Mostly people used bicycles instead of automobiles, rick-
shaws for taxis or the bus, and horse carriages for trucks.
Only a few cars were running when my grandfather was
little. He was the oldest brother of eight since his older sister
passed away before he was born. (He did not know exactly
what she had, but she was born with an illness.) His parents
owned a plaster company with about thirty employees, so
they had to keep an eye more on their employees than on
him. Because of this, my grandfather grew up without stress
or bad pressure from his parents. When he was in grade
school, he often climbed big trees and ran about two miles
around his neighborhood with his friends. He said he had
many good friends in school, and he loved to go to school
every day. Until the age of 11, he liked school and he also
liked to play soldiers with his friends. However, when he

entered junior high school, the educational system was turned into one of soldier preparation for World War II. This is when he started to hate going to school. His school started to teach all the students how to fight in the war, and his teachers started to act like corporals. He started taking kendo (one type of martial arts) when he was 12, and that kept him going to school. He said he went to school to play baseball and kendo with his friends, and he did not like school without these.

My grandfather was 21 years old when World War II began. He was frightened of going to war, but Japanese society did not allow him to express his feelings. He was taught that he had to feel great pleasure about being able to fight for his country. During the war, he was mostly in China. He was responsible for meals for soldiers, so, fortunately, he himself never starved. The weather in China was hard for him to deal with. During the winter, the temperature dropped down to minus 30C, and sometimes even the ocean froze. Someone who stayed outside for even a little while, would easily freeze to death. During the summer, it was 40C daytime and 3C at night. He said living in China was very rough.

At the beginning of the war, Japan was winning, so he was rarely in danger of getting killed. However, toward the end of this war, the U.S. started taking control, and he was often chased by American planes. He said that was the most frightening experience he has ever had. some of his friends became kamikazes when Japan saw there was no possibility of winning and decided to inflict as much damage on U.S. forces as it could before conceding defeat. Kamikaze pilots were drawn from the best pilots in Japan. Trained as usual at first, toward the end of the war they were commanded to become kamikazes. Some of them were sad and cried hysterically upon being chosen, and some were glad to be numbered among the elite. My mother told me that my grandfather looked upset when he was talking about the kamikazes since he lost some of his friends that way.

When the war was over, he went back home to his mother. She had been praying every night for him not to get shot, and she welcomed him with tears and a tight hug. The city where he grew up was bombed during the war, so there was nothing but some burned trees and burned houses when he went back. Until his parents finished building a new house, he had to stay in his relatives' houses. Fortunately, all of his relatives were kind and willing to take care of him.

He married my grandmother when he was 26 years old. A year later, my mother was born, and they moved to Tokyo. My grandfather helped his father's company and worked as an architect. He happened to see some American people in the city after the war, but he did not feel any hatred or any hostility toward them. However, he still has some dreams about the war, most of them about his frightening experiences.

My mother told me Americans bought her and other little kids candy and ice cream when she was young. I wondered how my grandfather felt when he saw Americans talking to his child. It turns out that he never saw my mother talking to them. He also said he was glad to know that I had many American friends here. When I went home last year, I told him that I was happy going to college in the U.S. and learning new things. Then he told me that he had no hatred toward the U.S., and he was very happy for me.

After this interview, I found out some things that I did not know. People in the U.S. think that kamikaze pilots were volunteers and willing to die for their country. But, the truth was different. Americans idealized the way Japanese soldiers fought in the war, and comprehended it in their own way. Only a few pilots chose to be kamikazes; the rest were chosen. The society did not allow them to voice anything against the country's decision. The image of kamikaze in the U.S. is one of courage and bravery, but Japanese people equate kamikaze with lack of freedom and sadness.

Regarding my grandfather's childhood, I had no idea that there were horse carriages in the city then because I associate Japan with tall buildings and automobiles. Tokyo, where I grew up, is one of the most advanced cities in the world today. I was surprised the city grew so fast. I couldn't even imagine that he had such a rough experience in his younger days because my grandfather is always so optimistic. After this interview, I have a new perspective on my grandfather, and I feel that I understand him better than before. And I was amazed by how rapidly Japanese society changed after World War II. Comparing his younger days and mine, I have a freedom that my grandfather did not have, and I have many more opportunities to voice my opinions. Through this interview, I learned not only about my grandfather but also about the changes in Japanese society.